PORTLAND

Like a Local

PORTLAND
Like a Local

BY THE PEOPLE WHO CALL IT HOME

Contents

EAT

DRINK

SHOP

ARTS & CULTURE

meet the locals

ALEX FRANE

Alex is a Portland native with no tattoos, which makes him something of a unicorn in the City of Roses. He makes up for it with his obsession with the city's bar and restaurant scene, and even stumbled into a career writing about it. Most days he can be found trying to pet neighborhood cats.

JENNI MOORE

Originally from Alaska, Jenni has lived in Portland for more than a decade, and loves exploring the city's food, arts, and culture as a journalist and photographer. On any given day she can be found eating a stellar brunch, browsing record stores, and attending awesome live music events.

PETE COTTELL

In 2013, Pete moved from Columbus, Ohio to Portland, to live in a van down by the river. After a year of #vanlife, he sold out and moved into a house. In his spare time you'll find him biking from one brewery to the next and listening to loud music in the crustiest bars possible.

Portland

WELCOME TO THE CITY

Oregon is famed for its snowcapped volcanoes, dark-green forests, and rugged beaches. And tucked away among all this eye-popping natural beauty, right on the banks of the winding Willamette River, is super-cool Portland. This is a city that's always shaking up the norms, which is no surprise for a place whose unofficial motto is "Keep Portland Weird." In fact, while almost every city and state in the US purports to live by one quirky slogan or another, in Portland they really are a kooky bunch. Here you'll find rogue taxidermists and bagpipe-playing unicyclists, bondage-wearing bartenders and tattooed comic book fans.

Countless free-spirited folks have been lured here over the years by the promise of such creative self-expression. Actually, there's a well-worn cliché about Portlanders: that none of them are actually from Portland. But whether born-and-bred or a transplant, locals

are united by their liberal views, unabashed individuality, and laid-back love of life. They're also all about community support, whether that's buying from local makers, sampling beers at a craft brewery, or picking up the latest read from an independent bookstores.

No wonder, then, that the city has such a friendly neighborhood feel. And that's where this book takes you. To the hip food cart where folks make friends in the line and the trendy coffee shop serving up locally roasted coffee, to the cozy bars fueling catch-ups over Oregon wines and the board game stores hosting friendly tournaments.

We can't pack all of Portland into these pages, but we can guarantee you'll find something special, whether you're a local looking to learn more about your city, or a visitor after inspiration for your first trip. So strap in, and get ready to explore Portland's creative and kooky heart.

Liked by the locals

"Portland likes to pretend it's a large city, but in reality it's a small town with big aspirations. There's a really strong community vibe here and locals try hard to support each other. Plus, put one foot out the door and you're guaranteed to bump into someone you know."

ALEX FRANE, FOOD AND DRINK WRITER

Costumed bike rides in summer, foodie festivals in fall, and festive fun in winter – there's always something afoot in Portland.

Portland
THROUGH THE YEAR

SPRING

ROSES IN BLOOM
Portland lives up to its "City of Roses" nickname come the spring, when these flowers blossom in parks and along sidewalks, filling the city with color and scent.

SHEBREW
Locals sip craft brews at this festival celebrating female-identified brewers and their beers and ciders. All proceeds go to the Human Rights Campaign, which advocates for LGBTQ+ equality.

TIME TO HIKE
As the days get warmer, Portlanders dust off their hiking boots and head to the Columbia River Gorge or Oregon coast to clear the cobwebs on a day hike.

SUMMER

ALFRESCO DINING
Patios around town swell with locals after a dose of blue skies and sunshine, while food cart pods are packed until late in the evening.

OREGON BREWERS FESTIVAL
Yep, it's another beer festival (this is Portland, after all). This five-day event is a summertime tradition for locals; here, they sample brews from over 90 craft breweries in leafy Tom McCall Waterfront Park.

BIKE TOWN
Summer sees a two-wheel takeover. Over 200 community-organized, themed bike rides take place during

month-long Pedalpalooza, while the World Naked Bike Ride sees locals saddle-up in their birthday suits to protest against dependency on fossil fuels.

AQUATIC ADVENTURES
When temperatures soar, locals make for the water, whether it's a paddle off Sauvie Island's sandy shores or a trip to the Oregon coast for a bit of surfing. The Big Float in July sees Portlanders bob down the Willamette River in a variety of colorful crafts, including inflatable inner tubes.

FALL

SWIFT WATCH
Every September, the lofty chimney of Chapman Elementary School is home to thousands of migrating swifts. At sunset, locals head here to watch these graceful birds dance through the sky before swooping down into the chimney to roost.

HARVEST FUN
Come fall, weekends are spent on Sauvie Island, getting lost in corn mazes and picking pumpkins to make spooky Jack O'Lanterns – all while dressed in flannel, of course.

FOODIE FESTIVALS
Portland's fall festivals are all about food. Fermentation Fest offers everything from kimchi to kombucha, The Wedge serves up local cheese, and Feast Portland celebrates the Pacific Northwest's bounty with grub from local and visiting chefs.

WINTER

FESTIVE LIGHTS
Portland lights up come Christmas – literally. Families admire the gaudily decorated houses along Peacock Lane, while friends gather to see Pioneer Courthouse Square's twinkling tree.

HITTING THE SLOPES
Thousands of wrapped-up Portlanders flock to the snowy slopes of Mount Hood each day to ski, snowboard, and sled the varied routes. There's always the chance for a hot cocktail or steaming mug of cocoa to warm up afterward, too.

PORTLAND MUSIC MONTH
Locals keep their spirits up in wet and dreary January with music – and lots of it. Portland Music Month sees hundreds of local musical acts performing at countless snug venues around town.

*There's an art to being a Portlander, from the dos and
don'ts of eating out to negotiating the city's streets.
Here's a breakdown of all you need to know.*

Portland
KNOW-HOW

For a directory of health and safety resources, safe spaces, and accessibility information, turn to page 186. For everything else, read on.

EAT
Portland is bursting with foodie spots, from cute bakeries to the city's famed food carts (of which there are many). Leisurely brunches are a weekend fixture, with places filling up early (get there before 10am to avoid lines). There's little need for reservations during the week, but they're a must on weekends, especially for upscale spots. Last thing: in true Portland style, the dress code is casual.

DRINK
The city's coffee scene is legendary, thanks to a clutch of local roasters and super-cool coffee shops. Locals often while away hours at cafés with a book or a laptop, topping up with refills when their caffeine levels get too low. As for alcohol, the scene is a mix of stylish bars, local breweries, and neighborhood dives. Whatever the vibe, most spots offer full food menus (by Oregon law, places serving liquor have to sell hot food) but be warned: in dives, this can mean a microwavable pie. Happy hours are offered by plenty of spots, often starting at 4pm.

SHOP
Portlanders love supporting local makers and crafting their own unique styles, so it's no surprise they prefer to shop at indie boutiques and vintage stores over malls and chain stores. On weekends, it's a good idea to get to vintage stores early if you want to grab the best finds.

Shops tend to open around 10am, with many not closing until 7 or 8pm (so 9-to-5ers can make it post-work). A heads up: while paper bags only cost 5 cents (single-use plastic bags are banned), make like a local and carry a tote.

ARTS & CULTURE

While most of Portland's independent galleries are free to enter, some of its museums and historic sights do charge an admissions fee (around $10). The city's historic movie theaters can get busy during the evenings, especially those that serve food and local brews (which many of them do), so book tickets in advance or arrive early.

NIGHTLIFE

Portland isn't big on nightclubs (by law, places serving alcohol need to have their last call at 2:30am). Instead, nights out are spent at comedy clubs, music venues, offbeat theaters, and – wait for it – strip clubs. There are more stripper joints per capita here than in any other US city, but these spots are more chilled out than sleazy, with locals of all stripes rocking up. Going-out attire is casual, but locals sometimes dress up for the theater.

OUTDOORS

On sunny days, Portlanders flock to the city's parks and river beaches to lounge, or strike out to nearby Columbia River Gorge to stretch their legs. Be sure to pick up your trash – pop it into trash cans in city parks or carry it home with you from trails – and don't make fires. Portland has a growing houseless population, with campsites found in some city parks and along roadways.

Keep in mind

Here are some more tips and tidbits that will help you fit in like a local.

» **Tip well** Adding 20 percent to your bill is a must at restaurants, bars, and food trucks.

» **Stay hydrated** Downtown has public drinking fountains (called Benson Bubblers) and tap water is on offer in bars and restaurants.

» **No smoking** Smoking is banned inside public buildings. While the purchase and use of cannabis is allowed, it is illegal to smoke it in public (although locals do light up the occasional joint in a park).

» **Stay dry** It's no joke: Portland can sure get rainy. Keep an umbrella or a rain jacket handy.

GETTING AROUND

While Portland doesn't have the most clearly defined neighborhoods (they tend to overlap), it can be roughly divided into six "quadrants": Northwest, Northeast, North, Southeast, South, and Southwest. Portland is built on a grid: numbered streets count the blocks west and east from the Willamette River (which splits the city in two), while named streets travel north and south from Burnside Street.

Once you learn the pattern, Portland is pretty easy to navigate. But to help you along, we've provided what3words addresses for each sight in this book, meaning you can quickly pinpoint exactly where you're heading.

On foot

Portland is amazingly walkable: sure, it's surrounded by hills, but most of the city is pretty flat. Plus, each block is shorter than the average US city block, meaning it's easier to find places to cross the road (as well as giving the city a more inter-connected feel). Pedestrian-friendly bridges like the Hawthorne and car-free Tillikum make crossing the river easy, too.

Portlanders are pretty laid-back, so walking tends to take a leisurely pace. That said, if you need to stop and check a what3words location, step to the side of the sidewalk. Walking is less fun when it rains (which can happen a lot), but don't let this put you off: just pull on some boots and a rain jacket like the locals and you're good to stroll.

On wheels

Portland is all about bicycles, with locals taking to two wheels for exercise, work commutes, nights out, and beyond. Many major streets have clearly marked bike lanes and bike parking, and there are more than 100 miles (160 km) of neighborhood greenways (low-traffic and low-speed streets where priority is given to cyclists and pedestrians) across the city. Be sure to follow all the rules of the road, such as obeying traffic signals, signaling when turning, and giving way to pedestrians. Cyclists need a front white light and a back red light or reflector when riding at night or in limited visibility. Wearing a helmet isn't a legal requirement for adults, but the majority of locals wear one whenever they hop on their bike, so follow their lead and stay safe.

BikeTown PDX, the city's bike-sharing scheme, has over 1,500 bright-orange cycles across the city. The bikes cost $1 to unlock (download the app to do this) and then cost 20 cents every minute from then on – so a 30-minute ride, for example, will cost $7 in total.
www.biketownpdx.com/homepage

By public transportation

Portland's primary public transit system, TriMet, makes getting around easy thanks to a fleet of buses and a light rail system, MAX. Portland Streetcar is another option, though it is limited to a few round-trip routes in the city center.

For buses and MAX, the easiest way to buy a ticket is by using the green contactless machines at MAX stations or on buses. Tickets for the streetcar can be bought by card, using machines on the platforms. For all of the above, 2.5-hour passes cost $2.50, while day passes are $5. If you're riding more frequently, download a Hop Card, which can be preloaded with funds or linked to cell phone payment apps. Tickets cover all three forms of transportation. *https://myhopcard.com*

By car or taxi

Between walking, cycling, and public transportation, there's no real need to travel by car in town. For longer jaunts, rideshares like Uber and Lyft are available. Cabs are less common, but if that's more your style, Radio Cab is a good option. Order cabs by phone or online.

If you do drive, be aware that the narrow streets in the inner part of the city are tricky to navigate and parking can be difficult.

Download these

We recommend you download these apps to help you get about the city.

WHAT3WORDS
Your geocoding friend

A what3words address is a simple way to communicate any precise location on earth, using just three words. ///ballots.future.quiz, for example, is the code for Portland's iconic bookstore Powell's. Simply download the free what3words app, type a what3words address into the search bar, and you'll know exactly where to go.

TRANSIT
All-purpose transit app

This multi-purpose transportation app provides bus and MAX times, routes, and trip planning, as well as options for rideshares like Uber and Lyft. It can also show you where to find BikeTown stations. Even better, it's straightforward and easy to use, making navigating the city a complete breeze.

Portland is a mosaic of overlapping neighborhoods, which nevertheless have their own character and community. Here we look at some of our favorites.

Portland
NEIGHBORHOODS

Alberta Arts District

During the latter half of the 20th century, creeping gentrification led to tensions in this historically Black neighborhood. While these issues remain, community groups have worked hard to revitalize the area with art: today, a mishmash of locals flock here to see Alberta's colorful street art, including pieces that recount the heritage of its Black community. {map 4}

Boise

Confusingly, locals don't call Boise by its official name. No, it's Mississippi to them, after one of its main drags. Come evening, a young crowd fills the patios of the area's laidback bars. {map 4}

Buckman

This buzzing patch is a major hipster hangout thanks to its craft breweries, music venues, and innovative restaurants. The area's west is also the location of a big houseless population. {map 3}

Clinton/Division

While actually made up of areas like Richmond and Hosford-Abernethy, this spot is often called after its main streets, Clinton and Division, which are dotted with cafés and restaurants. Little wonder so many young professionals live here. {map 3}

Downtown

Though post-pandemic Downtown isn't as bustling as it used to be, there's still plenty of life in Portland's city center, including indie stores and cool cafés. {map 1}

Foster-Powell

Affectionately nicknamed "Fo-Po" by locals, this rapidly developing area is the stomping ground of young families and first-time homeowners. It's also home to the Portland Mercado, a Latin American community center and food cart pod. {map 5}

Hawthorne

Thrifty Portlanders love this chi-chi hippie hub for its glut of vintage stores. Offbeat fashionistas can spend the whole weekend here, browsing for unique finds, before grabbing a bite in one of the relaxed restaurants. {map 5}

Jade District

Locals flock to this diverse district to fill up on pho, dim sum, Korean BBQ, and more. The district celebrates its varied communities at the Jade International Night Market every August, with shows including Mexican folk dances and Chinese dragon dances. *{map 5}*

Kerns

Much like its next-door neighbor Buckman, lively Kerns isn't short of places to eat, drink, and catch a gig. Locals often come here to make a night of it. *{map 3}*

Ladd's Addition

This leafy neighborhood is the haunt of older, affluent Portlanders, who live in its quaint Craftsman homes. Tourists pop by to see Ladd's wagon-wheel design; unlike the rest of gridded Portland, its streets branch out from a main roundabout. *{map 3}*

Laurelhurst

The turf of high-earning families, this pretty spot is famed for its palatial houses and verdant green spaces,

including the tree-dotted Laurelhurst Park. A large houseless encampment lies close to the park, creating a challenging juxtaposition of wealth and poverty. *{map 5}*

Mount Tabor

This neighborhood is a little out of most Portlanders' price range (it's one of the most expensive spots in the city). Instead, locals come here to run, cycle, and stroll through Mount Tabor Park, which blankets the huge volcanic cinder cone. *{map 5}*

Old Town/ Chinatown

The clue's in the name – or rather names. The city's birth-place in the mid-19th century, this area later became a busy Chinatown. Today, it's one of Portland's grittier spots and a great place for a night out thanks to its cool bars, queer clubs, and strip joints. *{map 1}*

Pearl District

Next door to Downtown, this district attracts an arty crowd who hang out in its cutting-edge galleries and chic boutiques. *{map 1}*

Sellwood-Moreland

Retirees and empty-nesters frequent the antique stores and venerable restaurants of these tree-lined, twin neighborhoods. *{map 6}*

Slabtown/ Nob Hill

Known as the Alphabet District to locals (thanks to its alphabetized street names), this trendy area is filled with indie bookstores and local makers' shops. *{map 2}*

St. Johns

Tucked away in North Portland, St. Johns feels like its own little village. It even has its own downtown, filled with cute coffee shops and bakeries, as well as a killer Mexican market and the entrance to the stunning St. Johns Bridge. *{map 6}*

Woodstock

New homeowners and students call this quiet, community-minded corner of Southeast Portland home. Locals adore its vintage shops, cute cafés, and beaut-iful historic homes. *{map 5}*

Portland
ON THE MAP

Whether you're looking for your new favorite spot or want to check out what each part of Portland has to offer, our maps – along with handy map references throughout the book – have you covered.

Sauvie Island

6

US-30

ST. JOHN

Willamette River

US-30

SOMERSET WEST

CEDAR MILL

FOREST GROVE

OR-8

HILLSBORO

US-26

ALOHA

OR-8

BEAVERTON

OR-217

TIGARD

OR-210

OR-99W

TUALATIN

I-5

| 0 kilometers | 5 | |
| 0 miles | | 5 |

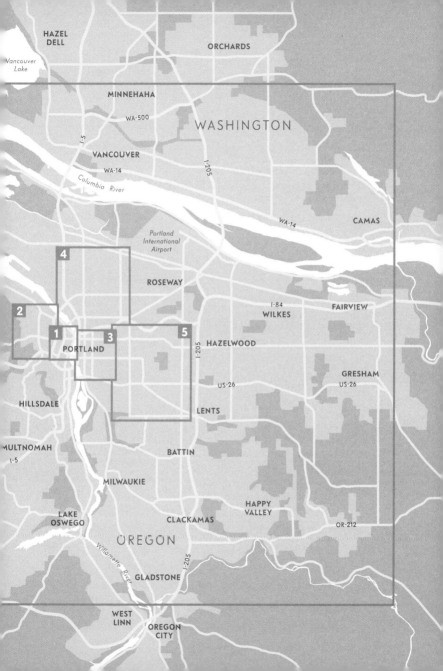

MAP 1

MAP 2

Willamette River

2

◗ Ladies of Paradise

Ⓓ Paymaster Lounge

PEARL DISTRICT

STREET

SW ALDER STREET

SW 14TH AVENUE

I-405

SW 11TH AVENUE

Portland State University

Ⓔ EAT

Eb & Bean *(p39)*
Farmer & the Beast *(p51)*
Langbaan *(p52)*

Ⓓ DRINK

Bar Diane *(p64)*
Breakside Brewery *(p71)*
M Bar *(p64)*
Paymaster Lounge *(p81)*

Ⓢ SHOP

Betsy and Iya *(p108)*
Daedalus Books *(p97)*
Ladies of Paradise *(p109)*
New Renaissance
  Bookshop *(p99)*
Roots & Crowns *(p92)*

Ⓐ ARTS & CULTURE

Cinema 21 *(p125)*
Freakybuttrue Peculiarium *(p134)*
Fuller Rosen Gallery *(p128)*
Pittock Mansion *(p117)*

Ⓝ NIGHTLIFE

Mox Boarding House *(p143)*

Ⓞ OUTDOORS

International Rose Test Garden
  (p166)
Portland Japanese Garden *(p164)*

MAP 3

 EAT

Berlu Bakery *(p36)*
Bomba PDX *(p39)*
Broder Café *(p33)*
Fermenter *(p47)*
Kachka *(p40)*
Le Pigeon *(p55)*
Mama Dút *(p44)*
Nong's Khao Man Gai *(p42)*
Nostrana *(p53)*
Plant Based Papi *(p45)*
Potato Champion *(p49)*
Quaintrelle *(p54)*
Ranch Pizza *(p42)*
Screen Door *(p32)*

DRINK

Bar Norman *(p65)*
Cascade Brewing *(p71)*
Coava Coffee Roasters *(p77)*
Dots Cafe *(p80)*
Enoteca Nostrana *(p66)*
Enso Winery *(p65)*
Kopi Coffee House *(p77)*
Loyal Legion *(p72)*
OK Omens *(p66)*
Palomar *(p63)*
Rimsky-Korsakoffee House *(p78)*
Rum Club *(p61)*
Sandy Hut *(p83)*
Scotch Lodge *(p63)*

SHOP

Banshee *(p107)*
Cargo *(p92)*
Guardian Games *(p89)*
Magpie Vintage *(p104)*
Scapegoat Tattoo *(p111)*

ARTS & CULTURE

Art Fills the Void *(p120)*
Attitude of Gratitude *(p121)*
Laurelhurst Theater *(p124)*
Nationale *(p130)*
National Hat Museum *(p134)*
OMSI After Dark *(p135)*
Radius Art Studio *(p130)*
Stark's Vacuum Museum *(p133)*

NIGHTLIFE

Aladdin *(p155)*
Clinton Street Theater *(p156)*
Crush Bar *(p148)*
Doug Fir Lounge *(p153)*
Funhouse Lounge *(p144)*
Helium Club *(p144)*
Revolution Hall *(p155)*

OUTDOORS

Eastbank Esplanade *(p169)*
SUP on the Willamette River *(p173)*

PIEDMONT

NE COLUMBIA BLVD
NE LOMBARD STREET

Woodlawn Park
WOODLAWN
NE DEKUM STREET

N ROSA PARKS WAY

Peninsula Park

Alberta Park

NE KILLINGSWORTH ST

Saraveza **D**

HUMBOLDT

Sweedeedee **E**

Mississippi Records **S**

ALBERTA ST

NORTH

Kee's Loaded Kitchen **E**

NE KILLINGSWORTH STREET

ALBERTA ARTS DISTRICT

Salt & Straw **E**

Les Caves **D**

Tin Shed **E**

Green Bean Books

Pine State Biscuits **S**

Booklover's Burlesque

Urdane **E**

Black United Fund Building **A** **N**

Alberta Rose Theatre **N**

NE PRESCOTT STREET

Prost! **D** N SKIDMORE ST

Matt's BBQ **E**

Interurban **D**

Gravy **E**

Pistils Nursery **S**

Paxton Gate **E**

Workshop Vintage **S**

BOISE

Mississippi Studios **N**

Bridge City Comics **S**

EEM **E**

N FREMONT ST

Irving Park

ALAMEDA

NORTHEAST

NE FREMONT STREET

ELIOT

NE KNOTT STREET

Bernstein's Bagels **E**

Women Making History in Portland **A**

Wonder Ballroom **E** **N**

Erica's Soul Food

Billy Ray's Dive **D**

Willamette River

Upright Brewing **D**

NE BROADWAY

Blossoming Lotus **E**

Twisted Croissant **E**

Hale Pele **D**

NE BROADWAY

LLOYD

Broadway Books **S**

SULLIVAN'S GULCH

NE MULTNOMAH STREET

Broadway Bridge

Cycle the 40-Mile Loop **O**

I-84

Culmination Brewing **D**

Hollywood Vintage **S**

KERNS

BANFIELD FREEWAY

NE SANDY BOULEVARD

Tropicale **D**

0 meters 800
0 yards 800

MAP 4

E EAT

Bernstein's Bagels *(p38)*

Blossoming Lotus *(p46)*

Doe Donuts *(p44)*

EEM *(p41)*

Erica's Soul Food *(p49)*

Gravy *(p34)*

Kee's Loaded Kitchen *(p41)*

Matta *(p48)*

Matt's BBQ *(p48)*

Pine State Biscuits *(p32)*

Salt & Straw *(p37)*

Sweedeedee *(p35)*

Tin Shed *(p33)*

Twisted Croissant *(p36)*

Urdaneta *(p54)*

D DRINK

Billy Ray's Dive *(p80)*

Culmination Brewing *(p68)*

Hale Pele *(p62)*

Interurban *(p61)*

Les Caves *(p66)*

Prost! *(p75)*

Saraveza *(p75)*

Tropicale *(p62)*

Upright Brewing *(p69)*

S SHOP

Bridge City Comics *(p91)*

Broadway Books *(p97)*

Green Bean Books *(p98)*

Hollywood Vintage *(p107)*

Little Axe Records *(p101)*

Mississippi Records *(p101)*

Paxton Gate *(p95)*

Pistils Nursery *(p93)*

Workshop Vintage *(p106)*

A ARTS & CULTURE

Black United Fund Building *(p123)*

Hollywood Theatre *(p127)*

Women Making History in Portland *(p120)*

N NIGHTLIFE

Alberta Rose Theatre *(p147)*

Booklover's Burlesque *(p158)*

Mississippi Studios *(p152)*

Wedgehead *(p143)*

Wonder Ballroom *(p152)*

O OUTDOORS

Cycle the 40-Mile Loop *(p173)*

KERNS

NORTHEAST

NE 28TH AVE

NE GLISAN ST

BANFIELD

NE 47TH AVENUE

FREEWAY

NE 60TH AVE

LAURELHURST

EAST BURNSIDE STREET

EAST BURNSIDE STREET

S Music
Millennium

O Laurelhurst
Park

SE STARK STREET

Zymoglyphic
Museum **A**

E Coqu

SUNNYSIDE

NE 49TH AVE

MOUNT
TABOR

SE BELMONT STREET

D Never Coffee

Movie Madness Video **A**

D Horse Brass Pub

House of
Vintage

HAWTHORNE

O Mount Tabor
Park

The Hazel Room **E S**

Jackpot Records **S S**

E Fried Egg I'm in Love

N QuarterWorld

SE 60TH AVENUE

SE HAWTHORNE BLVD

Red Light
Clothing Exchange

S E A The Bagdad Theater
& Pub

Harlow

SE 50TH AVENUE

SE 30TH AVENUE

SE CÉSAR E CHÁVEZ AVENUE

Kim Jong
Grillin'

She Bop **S**

Artifact: Creative
Recycle

RICHMOND

E Bete-Lukas

SE DIVISION STREET

E

S

SE DIVISION STREET

Clinton
Park

KaTi Portland

Third Eye Books,
Accessories & Gifts

SOUTH
TABOR

SE 52ND AVENUE

SOUTHEAST

N Baby Ketten Klub

SE POWELL BOULEVARD

SE POWELL BOULEVARD

SE 26TH AVENUE

BOULEVARD

Jojo **E**

CRESTON-
KENILWORTH

Creston
Park

Devils Point **N**

SE FOSTER ROAD

FOSTER-
POWELL

SE GLADSTONE ST

D

Kenilworth
Park

SE HOLGATE

BOULEVARD

SE HOLGATE

Portland
Cà Phê

REED

SE STEELE STREET

SE CÉSAR E CHÁVEZ AVENUE

Red Castle Games **S**

Reed
Canyon

Woodstock
Park

SE 52ND AVENUE

SE HAROLD STREET

0 meters   800

0 yards   800

WOODSTOCK

Red Fox **S**
Vintage

SE WOODSTOCK BLVD

MAP 5

E EAT

Bete-Lukas *(p40)*
Coquine *(p54)*
Fried Egg I'm in Love *(p35)*
Harlow *(p45)*
The Hazel Room *(p34)*
Jojo *(p51)*
KaTi Portland *(p46)*
Kim Jong Grillin' *(p51)*
Secret Pizza Society *(p47)*

D DRINK

Horse Brass Pub *(p72)*
Never Coffee *(p79)*
Portland Cà Phê *(p78)*
Roscoe's *(p73)*

S SHOP

Artifact: Creative Recycle *(p105)*
Crossroads Music *(p100)*
House of Vintage *(p106)*
Jackpot Records *(p100)*
Music Millennium *(p102)*
Red Castle Games *(p88)*
Red Fox Vintage *(p105)*
Red Light Clothing Exchange *(p104)*
She Bop *(p95)*
Third Eye Books, Accessories
   & Gifts *(p99)*

A ARTS & CULTURE

The Academy Theater *(p127)*
The Bagdad Theater & Pub *(p125)*
Movie Madness Video *(p135)*
Zymoglyphic Museum *(p132)*

N NIGHTLIFE

Baby Ketten Klub *(p140)*
Devils Point *(p157)*
QuarterWorld *(p141)*

O OUTDOORS

Laurelhurst Park *(p164)*
Mount Tabor Park *(p171)*

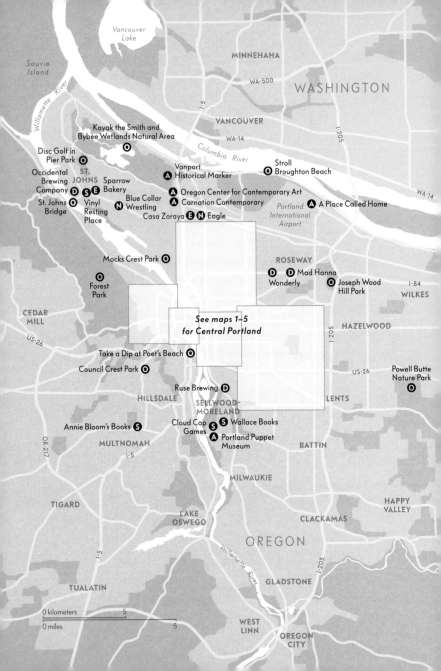

Vancouver Lake

MINNEHAHA

WA-500

WASHINGTON

VANCOUVER

WA-14

Columbia River

Sauvie Island

Willamette River

Kayak the Smith and
Bybee Wetlands Natural Area ⊙

Stroll ⊙
Broughton Beach

Disc Golf in
Pier Park ⊙

ST. JOHNS

Vanport Ⓐ
Historical Marker

WA-14

Occidental
Brewing
Company Ⓓ Ⓢ Ⓔ
Sparrow
Bakery

Oregon Center for Contemporary Art Ⓐ

A Place Called Home Ⓐ

St. Johns ⊙
Bridge
Vinyl
Resting
Place

Ⓝ Blue Collar
Wrestling

Carnation Contemporary Ⓐ

Portland
International
Airport

Casa Zoraya Ⓔ Ⓝ Eagle

Mocks Crest Park ⊙

ROSEWAY

Forest ⊙
Park

Ⓓ Ⓓ Mad Hanna
Wonderly

Joseph Wood ⊙
Hill Park

I-84

WILKES

CEDAR
MILL

See maps 1–5
for Central Portland

HAZELWOOD

US-26

Take a Dip at Poet's Beach ⊙

Council Crest Park ⊙

US-26

Powell Butte
Nature Park
⊙

Ruse Brewing Ⓓ

HILLSDALE

SELLWOOD-
MORELAND

LENTS

Annie Bloom's Books Ⓢ

Cloud Cap Ⓢ Wallace Books
Games

BATTIN

MULTNOMAH

I-5

Portland Puppet Ⓐ
Museum

OR-217

MILWAUKIE

TIGARD

LAKE
OSWEGO

HAPPY
VALLEY

CLACKAMAS

I-5

Willamette River

OREGON

GLADSTONE

TUALATIN

0 kilometers   5

0 miles   5

WEST
LINN

OREGON
CITY

MAP 6

6

CAMAS

A Nichaqwli
Monument

FAIRVIEW

N Edgefield

GRESHAM
US-26

OR-212

E EAT

Casa Zoraya *(p52)*

Sparrow Bakery *(p38)*

D DRINK

Mad Hanna *(p81)*

Occidental Brewing
Company *(p68)*

Ruse Brewing *(p71)*

Wonderly *(p60)*

S SHOP

Annie Bloom's Books *(p98)*

Cloud Cap Games *(p91)*

Vinyl Resting Place *(p102)*

Wallace Books *(p96)*

A ARTS &
CULTURE

A Place Called Home *(p123)*

Carnation Contemporary *(p129)*

Nichaqwli Monument *(p116)*

Oregon Center for Contemporary
Art *(p130)*

Portland Puppet Museum *(p132)*

Vanport Historical Marker *(p118)*

N NIGHTLIFE

Blue Collar Wrestling *(p156)*

Eagle *(p151)*

Edgefield *(p153)*

O OUTDOORS

Council Crest Park *(p171)*

Disc Golf in Pier Park *(p172)*

Forest Park *(p165)*

Joseph Wood Hill Park *(p168)*

Kayak the Smith and Bybee
Wetlands Natural Area *(p175)*

Mocks Crest Park *(p168)*

Powell Butte Nature Park *(p171)*

St. Johns Bridge *(p169)*

Stroll Broughton Beach *(p172)*

Take a Dip at Poet's Beach *(p175)*

EAT

Whatever type of grub you're after, Portland will probably have it. The city is bursting with global flavors thanks to its innovative restaurants and countless kick-ass food carts.

Brunch Spots

It's a stereotype but it's true: Portlanders love brunch,
enough to wait literally hours in line for it. And with
huge breakfast burritos and plates piled high with
golden waffles, any wait is definitely worth it.

PINE STATE BISCUITS

Map 4; 2204 NE Alberta Street, Alberta Arts District;
///backed.turns.payer; www.pinestatebiscuits.com

Craving a taste of home, three transplants from North Carolina
started making buttery homemade biscuits (savory scones to Brits).
And they were a resounding hit with Portlanders. At the weekend,
the bleary-eyed schlep it here for the Reggie: a towering stack of fried
chicken, cheese, and gravy perched atop those fluffy biscuits.

SCREEN DOOR

Map 3; 2337 E Burnside Street, Kerns; ///ticket.meal.hills;
www.screendoorrestaurant.com

If anywhere can tempt locals from their beds on a Sunday morning,
it's this legendary spot. And while all of the Southern-style grub here
is delicious, it's the golden waffles — stacked with fried chicken, and
drizzled with lashings of butter and syrup — that make lines form

Order brunch online ahead of time for take-out, then enjoy an alfresco lunch in leafy Lone Fir (p69).

around the block. This sacred brunch dish is so good that hungry punters will gladly travel across the city for it – leave now, and you might just get there first.

BRODER CAFÉ

Map 3; 2508 SE Clinton Street, Hosford-Abernethy;
///risen.plant.ample; www.broderpdx.com

This place helped kick off Portland's brunch craze back in 2007 – but it wasn't for serving your basic "avo on toast." Nope, it was Broder's minimalist take on Scandi classics that won them loyal legions of fans. Come here for open-faced gravlax sandwiches, egg-topped *lefse* (Norwegian potato crepes), and Swedish meatballs with lingonberry jam. After this, you'll never order avocado toast again.

» Don't leave without trying the *aebleskiver*. Many Portlanders admit to being a little addicted to these spherical little Danish pancakes, served with yummy lingonberry jam and powdered sugar.

TIN SHED

Map 4; 1438 NE Alberta Street, Alberta Arts District;
///civic.ripe.blocks; www.tinshedgardencafe.com

Dog owners on weekend walkies head straight for Tin Shed – often because their pups drag them there. At this long-standing brunch spot, there's an entire menu devoted to four-legged friends, including a chicken, salmon, and sweet potato bowl. Human? Nom on the pesto scramble or black bean and tofu bowl – between belly rubs, of course.

THE HAZEL ROOM

Map 5; 3279 SE Hawthorne Boulevard, Hawthorne;
///invest.legal.bend; www.thehazelroom.com

The Hazel Room oozes old-world charm, with its Victorian-house setting, dark-wood furniture, and antique teapots filled with aromatic brews. Retirees end their Sunday strolls here with bacon-and-egg breakfast sandwiches, while thrifty shoppers celebrate their finds from nearby House of Vintage *(p106)* with tea-based cocktails.

GRAVY

Map 4; 3957 N Mississippi Avenue, Boise;
///swear.feel.decide; www.gravyrestaurant.com

Everyone and their next-door neighbor knows Gravy. This wildly popular breakfast restaurant is lauded for its huge American comfort food breakfasts. No matter the day, the homey space is filled with a clutch of Portlanders, from gig-goers refueling after a night out to comic-book fans eagerly awaiting the newest graphic

Narrow, brick-lined Radar *(www. radarpdx.com)* is often over-looked in favor of its next-door neighbor, the ever-popular Gravy. Skip the line at the latter and grab a table at this underrated spot for an eclectic brunch: think braised brisket served with cornmeal pancakes or bluefish pâté with baguette.

novels (Gravy is just up the street from Bridge City *(p91)*). Try the brioche French toast or, if you're really hungry, grab the housemade veggie sausages with lashings of mushroom gravy.

FRIED EGG I'M IN LOVE

Map 5; 3549 SE Hawthorne Boulevard, Sunnyside;
///spike.cloak.slate; www.friedegglove.com

Love puns? Love eggs? Then Fried Egg I'm in Love will be music to your ears. This yolk-yellow spot serves up eggy, cheesy sandwiches with band-inspired punny names. We love the Egg Zeppelin and Free-Range Against the Machine, but it's the flagship Yolko Ono that really hits all the right notes – melted cheese, oozing yolk, and a housemade sausage patty, with a bit of pesto for an added touch. It's enough to make you sing (but please don't).

» Don't leave without adding a hash brown patty to your sandwich. It takes it from a simple pleasure to a crispy, oily, delicious indulgence.

SWEEDEEDEE

Map 4; 5202 N Albina Avenue, Humboldt;
///deflection.wasp.twin; www.sweedeedee.com

With plants dotting the shelves and vinyl playing on a vintage record player, Sweedeedee feels like popping round to a pal's place for brunch. Grab a table with your bestie and order up classic brunch grub with a twist, like the sweet brown rice porridge with cultured butter and fruit preserves (you'll thank us later). The best bit: unlike brunching at a friend's, you won't have to wash up.

Bakeries and Sweet Treats

Portland sure does have a sweet tooth. The city is packed with everything from cute bakeries offering tasty pastries to super-sweet ice-cream parlors serving up frozen delights – so go on, treat yourself.

TWISTED CROISSANT

Map 4; 2129 NE Broadway, Sullivan's Gulch;
///sting.reason.weeks; www.twistedcroissant.com

When Portlanders have a croissant craving that just won't quit, they hotfoot it to Twisted. Each fluffy delight on sale is the result of three days' hard work by the croissant-obsessed staff. Just one bite of these flaky, golden pastries and you'll be on croissant cloud nine.

BERLU BAKERY

Map 3; 605 SE Belmont Street, Central Eastside;
///truly.learns.submit; www.berlupdx.com

During the pandemic, chef Vince Nguyen was forced to close Berlu, his acclaimed restaurant. But then he got creative. Drawing inspiration from his Vietnamese roots, he set up a take-out bakery – and holy moly, it was an instant hit. So much so, in fact, that it's sticking around, even though his restaurant is once again up-and-running. Only open Sundays, this minimalist spot (now with in-house dining) is inundated with Buckman locals, who come here to snap pics of, and then quickly devour, the super-tasty colorful bakes. The vivid green pandan waffles are particularly sublime.

» **Don't leave without** booking in for dinner at Berlu restaurant to enjoy contemporary Vietnamese grub from the multicourse menu.

SALT & STRAW

Map 4; 2035 NE Alberta Street, Alberta Arts District;
///object.else.snaps; www.saltandstraw.com

Portland-born ice-cream chain Salt & Straw has a cult following. And with good reason: it serves up some of the most delicious ice cream you've ever eaten. The flavors are something else too; instead of vanilla, you'll find delicious concoctions like honey lavender, Arbequina olive oil, and – wait for it – pear and blue cheese. Grab a couple of scoops and prepare to get evangelical.

Try it!
CHOCOLATE TOURS

Take a tour of the factory at Candy Basket (www.candybasketinc.com), Portland's much-loved chocolatiers, to learn all about how it makes its tasty treats – and to gorge on fresh-off-the-line samples, of course.

BERNSTEIN'S BAGELS

Map 4; 816 N Russell Street, Eliot;

///edit.fakes.flank; www.bernsteinsbagels.com

Ask any Portlander where to find the best bagels in town and they'll point you to Bernstein's. Heck, they'll probably come with you. Slow-risen, hand-rolled, and then boiled, these dense-yet-light golden rings are utterly addictive, especially when paired with Bernstein's playful seasonal schmears, spiked with things like beetroot or spicy peppers.

SPARROW BAKERY

Map 6; 8195 N Lombard Street, Unit 101, St. Johns;

///trample.chattering.sandbags; www.thesparrowbakery.net

First thing in the morning, this cute spot in the leafy St. Johns neighborhood is packed with rushed commuters and test-weary students. Why? Because the menu of classic breakfast pastries is

Shh!

Run by Ada and Carla Chavez, pop-up bakery Kumare PDX serves up mouthwatering *ensaymadas*, a traditional Filipino pastry and the sisters' favorite childhood treat. These fully vegan doughy delights are a sort of cross between a cinnamon roll and a cupcake, with toppings like *ube* (purple potato) and dulce de leche. Locals in the know keep a constant watch on the website *(www.kumare.store)* to see where the bakery will be popping up next.

to die for. Battle through the crowds to grab a fluffy cardamon roll or buttery croissant, and then head to nearby Cathedral City Park to devour it, crumbs and all.

EB & BEAN

Map 2; 645 NW 21st Avenue, Nob Hill;
///taxi.taking.pass; www.ebandbean.com

Thanks to Eb & Bean, froyo has never felt less virtuous. This paired-back little shop serves up towering swirls of frozen goodness in some seriously decadent flavors, such as coffee caramel and hazelnut praline. To top it off (pun intended), you can get your froyo drizzled with sauce and sprinkled with toppings like iced oatmeal cookies. Who needs ice cream, anyway? (Sorry, Salt & Straw.)

» Don't leave without picking up one of the hand-packed froyo pints from the freezer – you'll thank us later.

BOMBA PDX

Map 3; 2128 SE Division Street, Hosford-Abernethy;
///shout.cover.entry

When he had some extra time during the pandemic, Scott Rivera decided to explore his Italian heritage. The result was Bomba PDX. Operating out of Scottie's Pizza Parlor (Rivera's main gig), this pop-up serves up indulgent *bomboloni*: "little bombs" of fried, sphere-shaped dough filled with things like lemon curd, vegan raspberry jam, and pistachio cream. If all this has you drooling, check out Bomba PDX's social media for the next time it'll be popping up at the parlor.

Comfort Food

*The perfect antidote to Portland's rainy days
(and, let's be honest, beer-filled nights), comfort
food is all about bringing friends and family together
over warming, soul-soothing dishes.*

BETE-LUKAS
Map 5; 2504 SE 50th Avenue #D, Richmond;
///grades.rank.memo; www.bete-lukas.com

A mix of beanie-topped vegans, besuited office workers, and suburban parents on a night off fills this low-lit dining room come evening. Why? For the finger-licking, plant-forward Ethiopian grub, of course. Join them for a hearty plate of *misser wot* (spiced lentils), served with an oh-so-satisfying injera (flatbread) for dipping. It's utter perfection.

KACHKA
Map 3; 960 SE 11th Avenue, Buckman;
///handle.moral.folds; www.kachkapdx.com

A child of Jewish Belarusian immigrants, Bonnie Morales wanted to share her family's cuisine with her Portland neighbors – so she opened Kachka. Today, boisterous groups of families and friends flock to this cozy spot for the tummy-filling Russian food. The stuffed dumplings

Love the dumplings? Visit the upstairs Lavka market, where you can grab frozen bags of them to take home.

are an obvious winner, but make sure you try the intriguingly named "herring under a fur coat" – this layered dish of herring, carrots, beets, and egg is simply delicious.

KEE'S LOADED KITCHEN
Map 4; 5020 NE Martin Luther King Jr. Boulevard, King;
///handy.themes.year

This bright-red hut may be small in size but it isn't in much else. Hungry North Portlanders swarm here for owner Kianua "Kee" Nelson's huge, heaped plates of soul food, which burst with rich flavors: think smoky beef brisket and crab-infused mac and cheese. Keep an eye on social media, where Kee posts about the menu (it changes daily) and if she's run out of food – which, with grub this good, happens a lot.

EEM
Map 4; 3808 North Williams Avenue Street #127, Boise;
///eggs.wicked.enjoy; www.eempdx.com

Eem is the Thai word for "satiated," which is a comically humble way to describe a meal at this Thai-BBQ fusion restaurant. The buzzy spot is constantly filled with what seems like half of the city, who come for the unorthodox riffs on Thai classics (we love the massaman curry with smoked pork). The Thai words for "bellyful of heaven" would also make a great name, but Eem will do for now.

» **Don't leave without** trying the signature dish: a creamy white curry teeming with smoky brisket burnt ends.

NONG'S KHAO MAN GAI

Map 3; 609 SE Ankeny Street C, Buckman;
///drove.poster.humble; www.khaomangai.com

Nong Poonsukwattana is a true entrepreneur. Arriving in the US with just $70, she quickly set up a food cart selling her take on *khao man gai*. This simple Thai dish of chicken and rice is raised to perfection by Nong's utterly addictive gingery sauce (it's a secret family recipe).

» Don't leave without listening to an episode of Nong's *Riding the Tiger* podcast, where she interviews other successful entrepreneurs.

RANCH PIZZA

Map 3; 2239 SE 11th Avenue, Ladd's Addition;
///shirts.units.tummy; www.ranchpdx.com

If dipping your pizza crust in ranch dressing is wrong, then Ranch Pizza doesn't want to be right. The indulgent dressing is an obligatory addition to the pizzeria's thick squares of pan pizza, topped with things like local veggies and chunky ricotta. Grab a slice and get dipping.

LUC LAC

Map 1; 835 SW 2nd Avenue, Downtown;
///many.notion.noses; www.luclackitchen.com

Yes, Old Portland grumps rag on Luc Lac for being popular with "the kids." But there's a reason why this late-night munchies spot is so hot: the well-priced, eat-till-you-pop Vietnamese grub. Join cash-strapped students and party goers from Old Town/Chinatown as they devour tangy bowls of warming pho and huge banh mi sandwiches.

Liked by the locals

"Nong's is one of those places that shows the beauty in doing something simple exceptionally well. The chicken is always gently poached, the rice infused with flavor, and the sauce – well, no wonder it has such a following."

BROOKE JACKSON-GLIDDEN,
EDITOR AT EATER PORTLAND

Veggie and Vegan

According to PETA, Portland is one of the best places in the US for vegan food, and its veggie scene ain't too shabby either. From fermented burgers to fluffy donuts, there's plenty to tempt.

DOE DONUTS

Map 4; 4110 NE Sandy Boulevard, Hollywood;
///tender.month.knots; www.doedonuts.com

Skip overrated Voodoo Doughnuts – Doe's is the place to be. This shop rustles up delicious gourmet donuts for hungry Hollywood locals. The best thing is, not only are the deep-fried bites totally vegan, they're also made using local and, where possible, organic, non-GMO, and fair-trade ingredients.

MAMA DÚT

Map 3; 1414 SE Morrison Street, Buckman;
///safely.line.wiping; www.mamadut.com

When COVID-19 struck, hairstylist Thuy Pham started making and selling vegan pork belly from her kitchen. The crispy-skinned goodness drove local vegans so wild, she was quickly able to open a brick-and-mortar restaurant selling her favorite Vietnamese dishes – all 100 percent vegan, of course. The place is always buzzing with plant-powered people, who pop by for plates of delicious chik'n fried oyster mushroom banh mi or pork belly steam buns.

» Don't leave without a bottle of one of Pham's incredible drinks, such as passion fruit limeade or Thai tea lemonade.

PLANT BASED PAPI

Map 3; 1412 SE Morrison Street, Buckman;
///prom.towns.entire; www.plantbasedpapi.com

Trying to convince your hardcore carnivore pals that vegan food is delicious? Take them to Plant Based Papi. One of Portland's buzziest vegan spots, this Black-owned restaurant (run by the Plant Based Papi himself, Jewan Manuel) offers some truly mind-blowing dishes. Highlights include the creamy truffle mac and cheese, loaded jackfruit tacos, and stacked burgers. Your friends might arrive dubious meat-eaters, but they'll leave plant-based converts.

HARLOW

Map 5; 3632 SE Hawthorne Boulevard, Hawthorne;
///plank.vase.lease; www.harlowpdx.com

A meal at Harlow feels wonderfully virtuous. Why? This café is dedicated to fresh, local, and completely gluten-free food. Here, lycra-clad yogies sip on smoothies, while hungry families munch their way through vegetable-packed scrambles. Our favorite is the stroganoff with wild seasonal mushrooms and tempeh – it's healthy, delicious, and fantastically filling.

BLOSSOMING LOTUS
Map 4; 1713 NE 15th Avenue, Irvington;
///names.boom.bowls; www.blpdx.com

Blossoming Lotus has been Portland's go-to vegan date spot for years. The high-ceilinged dining space is stylish yet cozy; the menu is diverse, with everything from a lentil-and-walnut cheeseburger to yakisoba noodles up for grabs; and the housemade craft cocktails keep the conversation flowing. Get ready to fall in love.

KATI PORTLAND
Map 5; 2932 SE Division Street, Richmond;
///jobs.entire.stole; www.katiportland.com

Southeast residents are big fans of this snug little Thai place. Its rustic decor, with dark wooden furniture and tin accent walls, is illuminated by green pendant lamps and a light-bulb sign stating "pad thai." And wow, what a pad thai it serves: thin rice noodles mixed with things

Shh!

Unless you're a Rose City Park local, you could easily miss Dirty Lettuce (*https://dirtylettuce. square.site*). And if you did, that would be a shame – especially for your stomach. At this humble spot, you can devour some of the most amazing vegan soul and Cajun food in all of Portland. The corn bread, fried catfish, collard greens, and red beans and rice are all delish, but it's the crispy chicken-fried seitan that really steals the show.

like tempeh, peanuts, and bean sprouts, all doused in a signature sauce. Other offerings include green curry with tofu, Thai street fried rice, and *pad kee mao* – and all are ask-for-seconds delicious.

» Don't leave without sipping on one of the refreshing vegan Thai iced teas (made with coconut milk instead of condensed milk).

SECRET PIZZA SOCIETY

Map 5; 7201 NE Glisan Street, Montavilla;
///slim.combining.being; www.secretpizzapdx.com

Despite the name, it's no secret these guys make the tastiest plant-based pies in town. And this is a task they take very seriously. All the dough is crafted in-house, as are the plant-based sauces and cheeses, so you don't have to worry about eating anything processed. Join Montavilla residents escaping their DIY to-do lists and snack on the standout Chalupa Batman, a zesty pie topped with fresh tomato, taco tofu meat, and housemade po'Fredo sauce.

FERMENTER

Map 3; 1403 SE Belmont Street, Buckman;
///nature.hunt.tiger; www.fermenterspirit.com

If your gut is in need of a reboot, Fermenter can help. Oh yes, stomach-friendly bacteria are front and center at this quirky Buckman café. Join health-minded hipsters and snack on kale and kraut salad, black bean soup drizzled with spicy fermented sauce, and miso-glazed burgers; there's even housemade kefir and kombucha to wash it all down. Happy stomach, happy human.

Food Carts

Thanks to their number and diversity, food carts are the beating heart of Portland's foodie scene. Whether at individual carts or multi-cart pods, locals come to explore new cuisines and hang out with their buddies.

MATT'S BBQ

Map 4; 4233 N Mississippi Avenue, Boise;
///pipes.sorry.raced; www.mattsbbqpdx.com

It might not look like much, but this little yellow food cart is massively popular. Run by pitmaster Matt Vicedomini, it serves the best ribs and brisket you'll find outside of Texas (think juicy, oak-smoked, and extra tender meats). On the weekends, flannel-clad locals hotfoot it here to grab heaped trays of pulled pork and spare ribs. Rise early to beat them to it – with grub this good, Matt's can often sell out before lunch.

MATTA

Map 4; 4311 NE Prescott Street, Beaumont;
///enjoy.cases.rated; www.mattapdx.com

When Richard Van Le, a first-generation Vietnamese-American, was growing up in San Jose, his *ba noi* (aka grandma) would rustle him up delicious Vietnamese food. Fast-forward 20 years, and Le and his wife Sophie are doing the same for hungry Portlanders. From their little cart next to a rustic wood-and-metal workshop, they serve up mouthwatering Vietnamese dishes with an American twist. The pick of the bunch is, of course, "Grandma's Special": sliced steak tossed with hand-cut fries and rice, topped with *nuoc cham* (fish sauce).

POTATO CHAMPION

Map 3; 1207 SE Hawthorne Boulevard, Buckman;
///making.exists.rounds; www.potatochampion.com

This colorful cart serves up Portland's tastiest Belgian-style fries. And these twice-fried delights sure do draw the crowds. At lunch, shoppers refuel here after a morning rummaging in Hawthorne's vintage stores, while come evening, revelers from nearby bars pop by for a carb-hit. Try the fries covered in cheese and gravy (Canadian poutine-style), or doused in satay sauce and smoky raspberry jam (trust us, it works).

ERICA'S SOUL FOOD

Map 4; 120 NE Russell Street, Eliot;
///given.mobile.news; www.ericassoulfood.com

All hail Georgia-transplant Erica Montgomery for bringing her take on Southern soul food to Portland – especially her lemon-pepper wings. Served Atlanta-style, they're deep-fried, sprinkled in lemon-pepper seasoning, and dripping with sauce (like jerk, toriyaki, or classic Buffalo). It's hardly surprising there's always a line outside.

» **Don't leave without** devouring some of Erica's other dishes, from shrimp and grits to smothered chicken to catfish sandwiches.

Solo, Pair, Crowd

Portland has more food carts than you can shake a stick at – even enough to cater for you, two, and the whole crew.

FLYING SOLO

Winner winner chicken dinner

FOMO's Korean chicken wings are two things: delicious and messy, especially if you're ordering them bone-in. Grab some all for yourself and indulge without anyone saying, "Erm, you've got sauce on your face."

IN A PAIR

Share the love

Stretch the Noodle offers the best Chinese noodles in town. Period. Even better, the portions are giant, so you can order one to share with a friend and have dollars left to buy some of the tasty dumplings.

FOR A CROWD

Make a speedy getaway

MidCity Smash Burger is one of the best places to grab a well-browned, juicy patty. The lines move quickly, so it's a good place to come with a group – it'll be just minutes before you're all chomping on a burger.

FARMER & THE BEAST
Map 2; 1845 NW 23rd Place, Slabtown; ///counts.zone.props;
https://farmer-and-the-beast.square.site

Nestled among Nob Hill's pod of food carts, forest-green Farmer & the Beast is the go-to spot for Portland carnivores looking to satisfy their smashed burger addiction. Here, these thin, crispy burgers are doused with melted cheese and topped by fresh iceberg lettuce.

KIM JONG GRILLIN'
Map 5; 4606 SE Division Street, Richmond;
///spins.card.duty; www.kjgpdx.com

If there was a prize for Portland's best-named food cart, Kim Jong Grillin' would win it hands down. And it'd probably win the prize for the city's most mouthwatering Korean food, too. Laid-back Sunday strollers are often led here by their stomachs, which growl hungrily for the cart's heaped helpings of bulgogi beef and yummy bibim boxes.

JOJO
Map 5; 3582 SE Powell Boulevard, Creston-Kenilworth;
///loser.fast.plan; www.jojopdx.com

Sure, Jojo's location isn't classy (it's plonked in an unassuming parking lot) but the food is outstanding. Hungry Portlanders gladly travel for its drool-worthy jojos (aka potato wedges) and huge fried chicken-thigh sandwiches, topped with things like pickles and Alabama white sauce.
» Don't leave without checking out Jojo's iconic social pages: run by owner Justin Hintze, they're random, chaotic, and utterly hilarious.

Special Occasion

Birthday? Date night? Payday? Any and all occasions are marked with a meal in this food-obsessed city. But don't expect white tablecloths here – this is laid-back Portland, after all.

CASA ZORAYA

Map 6; 841 N Lombard Street, Piedmont; ///purple.basin.glitz;
www.casazorayapdx.com

Having a family reunion? Head here. Not only does this family-run spot serve up fresh Peruvian dishes that are perfect for sharing, it also has welcoming vibes (owner Zoraya Zambrano and her two kids will make you feel like one of the gang). Top tip: the ceviche is super-fresh and delicious, so order plenty of it to avoid fighting over the last bite.

LANGBAAN

Map 2; 1818 NW 23rd Place, Slabtown; ///reject.drank.traded;
www.langbaanpdx.com

Snug Langbaan sure is popular for dates. In this intimate, 24-seat restaurant, couples old and new clink glasses beneath the soft glow of filament bulbs, before eating their way through the incredible multicourse Thai tasting menu. There's lots to love here, from the

Be sure to make a reservation as soon as possible, as Langbaan can book up months in advance.

aromatic swordfish in rice soup to the ground pork salad. Plus, what better way to end a date than with one of the elaborate desserts – they're made to impress.

NOSTRANA

Map 3; 1401 SE Morrison Street, Suite 101, Buckman;
///send.hops.doors; www.nostrana.com

It's all about Italian home cooking at Nostrana. Under a vaulted ceiling, friends toast payday over glasses of wine, then devour well-earned wood-fired pizzas and heaped bowls of sauce-laden pasta. Yes, it's a little pricey, but the food is delicious, the portions are generous, and the vibe is buzzing. What are paydays for?

MÅURICE

Map 1; 921 SW Oak Street, Downtown;
///square.ruins.unity; www.mauricepdx.com

This teeny pastry luncheonette takes minimalist to a whole new level; inside, almost everything is snow-white. But while the decor is kept basic, the food is far from it, with an ever-changing menu of Franco-Nordic dishes up for grabs. Downtown shoppers pop by here on the regular, but we recommend coming for a birthday lunch with the bestie. Celebrate with delicious dishes like mussels with tarragon and leeks, then finish up with a pastry – it's better than any birthday cake.
» Don't leave without grabbing a slice of the black pepper cheesecake with vanilla sable – it's totally divine.

URDANETA

Map 4; 3033 NE Alberta Street, Alberta Arts District;
///many.fruit.sits; www.urdanetapdx.com

Walking into this dark, rustic restaurant feels like stepping into a rural Basque inn; numerous worn pots and pans hang above the exposed kitchen and wine glasses line the shelves expectantly. Big gangs of friends congregate around the wooden tables to catch-up over endless plates of pintxos – all with a sherry in hand, of course.

COQUINE

Map 5; 6839 SE Belmont Street, Mount Tabor;
///gather.odds.tuck; www.coquinepdx.com

Portlanders looking to impress their other half's parents have Coquine on speed dial. Nestled in the leafy Mount Tabor neighborhood, this stylish bistro is all about Northwest dishes made with fresh, seasonal ingredients. Recommend the simple roasted chicken to your in-laws, followed by the smoked almond chocolate chip cookies – they'll be so impressed, they'll be offering to pay (well, maybe).

QUAINTRELLE

Map 3; 2032 SE Clinton Street, Hosford-Abernethy;
///cove.hulk.living; www.quaintrelle.co

With a golden chandelier, tiny marble bar, and bright modern art, this stylish spot wows right from the off. And the Pacific Northwest-inspired food isn't bad either: in fact, each locally sourced, seasonal dish is as much a piece of art as the room itself. Expect a pretty mixed crowd here, from plaid-wearing outdoorsy types celebrating promotions to comedy lovers treating themselves to a pre-show meal before ambling off to nearby Funhouse Lounge *(p144)*.

» **Don't leave without** trying the stunning cocktails from bar maven Camille Cavan, made with rare liqueurs and elaborate garnishes.

LE PIGEON

Map 3; 738 E Burnside Street, Kerns;
///ocean.shadow.award; www.lepigeon.com

An upscale French bistro with a Portland twist – that's Le Pigeon. This famous fine-dining spot offers haute cuisine, but it's not your usual French fare. Instead, chef Gabriel Rucker (a tattooed Californian who often cooks wearing a baseball cap) serves up a playful take on modern French and New American cuisine, all in a laid-back red-brick dining room. The decadent tasting menu includes things like tartare topped with anchovy aioli and a dessert of foie gras profiteroles (yes, you read that right). Now you know where to blow your bonus.

Try it!
COOK UP A STORM

Planning to make a special dinner at home? Portland Cookshop offers a range of cookery classes, many of them run by the region's most celebrated chefs *(www. portlandcookshop.com/classes)*.

SOUTHEAST 30TH AVENUE

Sewallcrest Park

SOUTHEAST HARRISON STREET

SOUTHEAST

Kick things off at LITTLE T BAKERY

Grab a fresh-out-of-the-oven croissant or fluffy baguette at this neighborhood favorite, which sources its ingredients from local Oregon growers and purveyors.

Grab a spot of lunch from KATI

Devour green curry with tofu or pad thai with tempeh at this all-vegan Thai restaurant. The portions are big and the Thai-inspired craft cocktails delicious.

1 SOUTHEAST **3** DIVISION STREET

2 SOUTHEAST CLINTON STREET

Cook up a storm with PORTLAND COOKSHOP

Join one of the classes run by celebrated local chefs and learn how to make everything from Mexican *conchas* to Japanese *onigiri* – and then taste the results.

SOUTHEAST 33RD AVENUE

Every summer the **Division-Clinton Street Fair** *arrives on Clinton Street, with live music and countless tasty foodie stalls.*

0 meters   250
0 yards   250

A foodie morning around
SE Division Street

It's a fact: Portlanders are all about their food. Weekends in the city are spent having long, lazy brunches, perusing farmers' markets and co-ops for super-fresh, locally grown produce, and catching up with friends at laid-back restaurants. And where better to enjoy an eating odyssey than SE Division Street and its neighbor Clinton Street? These dual avenues are liberally sprinkled with an abundance of much-loved restaurants and cafés. Join locals and spend a morning grazing your way around this foodie area.

**Save room for
PINOLO GELATO**
End your foodie odyssey with a scoop or two of Italian-style gelato made with local fruit. Make sure you grab a pint (or three) to take home with you, too.

1. Little T Bakery
2600 SE Division Street, Hosford-Abernethy; www.littletbaker.com
///heap.humid.softly

2. Portland Cookshop
2627 SE Clinton Street, Hosford-Abernethy; www.portlandcookshop.com
///treat.plots.limit

3. KaTi
2932 SE Division Street, Richmond; www.katiportland.com
///jobs.entire.stole

4. Pinolo Gelato
3707 SE Division Street, Richmond; www.pinologelato.com
///text.artist.posed

Division-Clinton Street Fair ///wool.margin.stews

DRINK

Breweries, wine bars and coffee shops are the lifeblood of Portland, where time is spent putting the world to rights over a beer or getting creative with a flat white in hand.

Cocktail Joints

Portland's cocktail scene is booming thanks to a slew of expert mixologists inspired by the city's creative spirit (and high-proof spirits). Sip on their inventive concoctions at these super-cool cocktail joints.

TEARDROP

Map 1; 1015 NW Everett Street, Pearl District; ///desks.wiring.atoms; www.teardroplounge.com

Before Teardrop, Portlanders much preferred sipping local brews to fancy cocktails. But that all changed in 2007 when this pioneering joint burst onto the scene with its expertly mixed creations. Today, the low-lit, industrial bar is packed nightly with gussied-up locals sampling from the ever-changing menu. Every drink is a winner, but for something unique, go for the seasonal cocktails.

WONDERLY

Map 6; 4727 NE Fremont Street, Beaumont; ///data.preoccupied.caged; www.wonderlypdx.com

A favored spot for locals of the sleepy Beaumont neighborhood, Wonderly keeps things simple. This modernist bar is all about fuss-free classic and original cocktails, built with aplomb and served in stylish surrounds (look out for the gilded stools). In the evenings, gossiping friends sip on "one-and-a-half-sized" martinis served in vintage-style glasses, while young parents on a night off go straight for the gin-tastic "Mommy's Thyme Out" (even the dads).

INTERURBAN

Map 4; 4057 N Mississippi Avenue, Boise;
///long.asset.leads; www.interurbanpdx.com

Chic cocktail lounge this is not. Instead, this laid-back spot offers a down-to-earth rustic vibe (we're talking mounted animal heads and unfinished wood) and fast food (give us a sloppy joe). But this doesn't mean the drinks lack class: the ever-changing cocktail menu always offers something intriguing, whether it's a smoky mezcal libation spiked with an obscure liqueur or a hearty whiskey drink.

RUM CLUB

Map 3; 720 SE Sandy Boulevard, Buckman;
///faced.pets.serves; www.rumclubpdx.com

At first glance Rum Club could be any old neighborhood watering hole, with its dark ambience, somewhat poppy music, and crowds of raucous industry workers shooting the breeze. But dig a little deeper and you'll discover the best rum-focused cocktails in the city (it is called Rum Club, after all). Our favorite? The punchy Celeste Swizzle, made with four Jamaican rums and a spot of absinthe.

» Don't leave without asking one of the bartenders to rustle you up a unique daiquiri; they're made with the drinker's specific tastes in mind.

HALE PELE

Map 4; 2733 NE Broadway, Sullivan's Gulch;
///lions.unrealistic.jump; www.halepele.com

This tiny tiki bar is fully committed to the kitsch: think decorative mugs, volcano sound effects, and a thatched roof. It's the perfect antidote for weather-beaten locals pining for a bit of sunshine (read: cursing Portland's rainy climate). Come the weekend, they hotfoot it here (dressed in tropical shirts, of course) to drink rum-laced fruity cocktails and pretend they're on holiday in the South Pacific.

TROPICALE

Map 4; 2337 NE Glisan Street, Kerns; ///inch.odds.fled; www.tropicale.co

This colorful bar is a testament to the joy and energy of Alfredo Climaco, one of Portland's most-loved bartenders. Raised in Puebla, Mexico, Climaco started off selling piña coladas at outdoor events around the city – and Portlanders went wild for them. In fact, they proved so popular that, in 2020, he was able to find a permanent

Craft cocktail connoisseurs looking to escape the crowds hurry over to Free House (www. freehousepdx.com). Nestled on a leafy street in North Portland, this rustic bar is beloved for its laid-back vibe and super-cute patio. Oh, and for serving up high-end drinks without the high price tag.

Having a house party? Tropicale sells its famed piña colada mix to-go for at-home mixing.

home for Tropicale. Sadly, Climaco passed away in early 2021, but his memory lives on through this colorful bar, where you'll find the best piña coladas in town.

SCOTCH LODGE

Map 3; 215 SE 9th Avenue #102, Buckman;
///tonic.follow.scan; www.scotchlodge.com

As you'd expect, this sultry, semi-subterranean bar is more than a little scotch obsessed, with hundreds of bottles of the stuff lined up behind the bar. But the whiskey here isn't often drunk neat – instead, it's expertly blended with housemade ingredients to create some truly stunning cocktails. Here, whiskey obsessives nurse boozy old fashioneds, while groups of 20-somethings snap pics of the belle-epoque decor in between sips of smoky scotch daiquiris.

PALOMAR

Map 3; 959 SE Division Street #100, Hosford-Abernethy;
///tuck.began.donor; www.barpalomar.com

Helmed by award-winning bartender Ricky Gomez, Palomar channels the raucous daiquiri bars of Miami, with its tropical wallpaper and constantly churning slushy machines. Join cheery friends as they descend on this fun spot to sup on some of the city's best daiquiris or sample "tweaked" classics, like a pineapple-spiked gin and tonic.

>> **Don't leave without** devouring some stomach-lining Cuban snacks, such as fried plantains, fritters, and *cubanos* (Cuban sandwiches).

Wine Bars

With the lauded Willamette Valley and up-and-coming Columbia River Gorge winelands a stone's throw away (take that, California), Portland is home to both world-class vintages and top-notch wine bars.

BAR DIANE

Map 2; 2112 NW Irving Street, Unit 105, Nob Hill;
///maple.dated.banana; www.bardiane.com

Looking for Portland's most stylish wine bar? This is it. Owned by Sami Gaston, who previously worked as an artist and designer, this intimate spot is an eclectic mix of exposed concrete, warm wood, and wine-hued walls. On any given evening, you'll find young couples sipping on crisp muscadets, while best buds sample funky pet nats (sparkling wine) and snap endless photos for their socials.

M BAR

Map 2; 417 NW 21st Avenue, Nob Hill;
///silent.arrive.jokes; www.mbarpdx.net

This chilled pocket wine bar (it's the smallest in Portland) is a great spot for dates thanks to its snug, candlelit ambience. Order a couple of glasses of one of the Old World wines and we guarantee

Waiting for your next paycheck? Head to M Bar between 4 and 5pm everyday for happy hour.

the conversation will be flowing all night. Date not a big wine fan? No problem – M Bar also serves up sake, cider, and craft beers.

ENSO WINERY

Map 3; 1416 SE Stark Street, Buckman; ///throw.local.pepper; www.ensowinery.com

Housed in a converted garage, Enso feels more like a mellow hipster coffee shop than your usual wine bar. Everyone from relaxed retirees to trilby-wearing creatives flocks to this industrial-style space to kick back in the mismatched chairs. And what are they drinking? Enso's housemade wines, of course. This chilled spot isn't just a bar; it's also a small-scale winery that produces some excellent vintages.

BAR NORMAN

Map 3; 2615 SE Clinton Street, Hosford-Abernethy; ///tiles.hoot.gates; www.barnorman.com

Focusing on natural wines, this snug bar is packed nightly with budding oenophiles who want to learn about what they're sipping. The staff here are total wine buffs, and can chat about everything from the producer to the bottle design. It's no surprise, though – the bar is owned by Portland's very own wine maven Dana Frank, an award-winning sommelier. Get ready to take notes.

» **Don't leave without** checking out the events schedule, which includes wine socials for women, trans, and nonbinary people.

LES CAVES

Map 4; 1719 NE Alberta Street, Alberta Arts District;
///issue.vibrates.frosted; www.lescavespdx.com

Okay, Les Caves is owned by local winemakers, but that doesn't mean it's all about Oregon vintages. In fact, this subterranean bar celebrates wine from around the world, with a focus on unusual vintages. Sip on Slovenian rosé, Serbian orange wine, or 20-year-old Spanish sherry beneath the warm glow of filament bulbs.

» Don't leave without trying a glass of one of the owners' wines – look out for Golden Cluster and Ovum on the menu.

OK OMENS

Map 3; 1758 SE Hawthorne Boulevard, Ladd's Addition;
///towers.darker.pencil; www.okomens.com

You caught us: this is a bistro, not a bar, but its wine menu is so good, we couldn't miss it off the list. Here, famed Portland sommelier Brent Braun flexes his wine credentials, serving up everything from refined rieslings to rare bottles from Napa (often priced absurdly low).

ENOTECA NOSTRANA

Map 3; 1401 SE Morrison Street, Suite 105, Buckman;
///ledge.crush.limbs; www.enotecanostrana.com

Geometric floors, Art Deco pieces, and a massive floor-to-ceiling glass wine cellar: this bar has got the wow-factor. Every evening, Buckman locals perch on the champagne cork-shaped bar stools and sample their way through a kick-ass collection of mostly Italian wines.

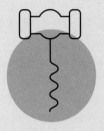

Liked by the locals

"One of the best things about Portland is our proximity to one of the best wine-growing regions in the world. But if the 40-minute drive to wine country feels too long, no worries – the city is full of fantastic wine bars and city wineries."

DANA FRANK, OWNER OF BAR NORMAN

Breweries

Other US cities might boast about having the best
and biggest craft brewery scene in the country – but
in Portland it's actually true. Don't believe us?
Explore "Beervana" and find out for yourself.

OCCIDENTAL BREWING COMPANY

Map 6; 6635 N Baltimore Avenue #102, St. Johns;
///rules.purchasing.spilt; www.occidentalbrewing.com

Portland is often portrayed as a haven for flannel-wearing, IPA-obsessives. And while not everyone in the city wears checked shirts, it's an undisputed fact that locals love hoppy beers. That's what makes brewmasters Ben and Dan Engler's choice to renounce them for clean, crisp European beers all the braver. But it worked: Portlanders (flannel-clad or otherwise) are big fans of their fresh altbiers and kolsches.

CULMINATION BREWING

Map 4; 2117 NE Oregon Street, Kerns; ///freed.fades.milky;
www.culminationbrewing.com

Of course there are crowd-pleasing IPAs on the menu here – this is Portland. But it's this cool microbrewery's offbeat, inventive beers that really draw the crowds. Try a mushroom-and-cocoa nib stout (it's basically a yummy, drinkable dessert) or sample one of the small-batch beers that have been aged in old gin and aquavit barrels. Unusual, we know, but it works.

» Don't leave without sampling Phaedrus, the brewery's most popular IPA (and deservedly so).

UPRIGHT BREWING

Map 4; 240 N Broadway, Rose Quarter; ///maple.random.rigid; www.uprightbrewing.com

Ask Portland's brewers where they're drinking tonight and the answer will be unanimous: Upright. Beer-makers sidle over to this industrial-style spot (known among their kind as the best brewery in the city) to spend the night drinking quality farmhouse ales, each batch lovingly crafted by brewmaster supreme Alex Ganum. After a few sips of a flavor-packed saison or wild ale you'll wonder why Upright's newly upgraded taproom still feels like a secret – but why ruin a good thing by blabbing about it on social?

Leafy Lone Fir Cemetery (649 SE 26th Avenue) is home to the little-visited tomb of George Frederic Bottler, a brewer who helped kick-start the city's beer movement in the mid-19th century. Legend has it that he smuggled some of the first hop strains into the Northwest, before Oregon was even a state.

Liked by the locals

"Craft beer is the norm in Portland. In fact, it's difficult to find a bar that doesn't have most of its beer list dedicated to local brews. Craft beer is also in every corner store, grocery store, and dive bar in the city. So when you say beer in Portland, you actually mean craft beer."

BEN EDMUNDS, HEAD BREWER AT BREAKSIDE BREWERY

RUSE BREWING

Map 6; 4784 SE 17th Avenue, Brooklyn; ///elbow.wanted.before;
www.rusebrewing.com

It's true: Ruse is a magnet for IPA diehards, who come to sip on the
brewery's juicy hazies and fervently discuss grain builds. But don't worry
if you know zilch about hop profiles; there are plenty of casual drinkers
here, too, lured by the promise of live music and a varied brew menu.

BREAKSIDE BREWERY

Map 2; 1570 NW 22nd Avenue, Slabtown;
///music.feeds.over; www.breakside.com

There's a lot to love about Breakside: its glistening Slabtown taproom,
its varied, constantly changing menu, and its award-winning IPAs.
But the best thing? The menu is miraculously free of misses, making
Breakside a great place to get sampling. Fittingly, the brewery's motto
is "seek and enjoy." So go on then, let's try another one.

CASCADE BREWING

Map 3; 939 SE Belmont Street, Buckman; ///star.medium.cherry;
www.cascadebrewingbarrelhouse.com

Hop-laden IPAs are banned at Cascade; instead, this unorthodox
brewery crafts funky sour ales. Try the vanilla and cinnamon tones of
the (somewhat unfortunately named) Bourbonic Plague or the cherry
burst and vinegar tang of Kriek, the brewery's most lauded beer.
» Don't leave without browsing the selection of to-go bottles;
it contains oddball brews that don't always make it onto the draft list.

Tap Houses and Brewpubs

It's not just breweries that make Portland a magnet for beer lovers – there are countless tap houses and brewpubs, too. Serving up an array of options, these spots are great places to sample the city's many brews.

LOYAL LEGION

Map 3; 710 SE 6th Avenue, Buckman; ///double.pigs.estate; www.loyallegionpdx.com

This sprawling bar is rightly named: the nearly 100 taps here only pour Oregon-made brews. Grab one of the blue leather booths and set off on a boozy, one-stop tour of the state's diverse brewery and cider scene, helpfully chauffeured by expert bartenders, of course.

HORSE BRASS PUB

Map 5; 4534 SE Belmont Street, Sunnyside; ///mixed.grace.sticky; www.horsebrass.com

Many of the clientele at the Horse Brass Pub have been coming here since the 1980s, and no wonder – this bar is a Portland institution. A sprawling British-style pub (think exposed beams, a hodgepodge of wooden tables, and beermats stuck above the bar), it played a key role in setting off Portland's monumental beer scene, being one of the first tap houses to serve local microbrews. Head here to enjoy its cask ales and hearty pub food, like Portland's best Scotch egg.

» **Don't leave without** challenging your pals to a game of darts for that proper British pub experience.

ROSCOE'S

Map 5; 8105 SE Stark Street, Montavilla; ///shaped.quest.dress;
www.roscoespdx.com

What do bikers, ski bums, and beer nerds have in common? They all hang out at Roscoe's. This beloved neighborhood dive – with its creaky floorboards and barely legible chalkboard menu – attracts an eclectic crowd thanks to a laid-back vibe and great beer list. The 20-ish handles pour out brews from big names like pFriem and Breakside (p71), as well as pleasant surprises from little guys like de Garde and Holy Mountain. The bar serves up big – and delicious – helpings of hearty Cajun food, too.

Try it!
BREW UP A STORM

Fancy making your own beer? Unicorn Brewing (www.portlandubrew.com) runs sessions every weekend where, with a little help from an expert brewer, you can make any style of beer you'd like from scratch.

Solo, Pair, Crowd

Whether you're heading out solo or with a group of buddies, "Beervana" welcomes all with its tasty brews.

FLYING SOLO
Beer with a book

Looking for a quiet night with a book in hand? Neighborhood watering hole Alberta Street Pub has plenty of cozy seating areas. Plus, if you grow tired of your novel, you can catch a stand-up show or live music performance.

IN A PAIR
Get romance brewing

Take your beer-obsessed date to the Tiny Bubble Room. Here, you can grab one of the individual cabanas for some privacy and enjoy tasty brews from the bar's 30 taps.

FOR A CROWD
Patio parties

Not only does Apex sport a huge collection of beers on draft and in bottles, but it also rocks a pretty massive patio that's perfect for groups, especially on a summer evening.

SARAVEZA

Map 4; 1004 N Killingsworth Street, Humboldt;
///ages.milky.firmly; www.saraveza.com

Founded by Midwest transplants, this casual bar usually harbors
more than a few Wisconsinites, especially when a Packers game is
on. But it's not just homesick Midwesterners that descend on this
spot on the regular. Thanks to its massive collection of bottled beers,
large tap list, and quirky decor (get ready for the mounted taxidermy
and a bottle-cap topped bar), Saraveza is a hangout for all sorts
of Humboldt locals. Plus, you definitely don't have to be from the
Midwest to appreciate the hearty bar food, which includes pasties
and the city's best squeaky cheese curds.

PROST!

Map 4; 4237 N Mississippi Avenue, Boise;
///torch.apple.exile; www.prostportland.com

While other Portland taprooms are all about Oregon beers, this
small bar celebrates Germany's brews – no surprise, given its name.
There's a mind-boggling array of imported lagers and ales on offer
(all German, of course), plus a good menu of traditional bites (we'll
have a pretzel, thanks). Regulars hunker down inside the rustic,
lumber-heavy interior – which echoes the vibe of a traditional
Germanic watering hole – while beanie-topped hipsters sporting
tattoos lounge on the fairy-light-strewn patio.

» Don't leave without ordering a massive Munich-beer-hall-style
**glass boot, filled with your favorite German brew (you'll definitely
need to share it with a friend).**

Coffee Shops

Coffee and beer are tied neck-and-neck for Portlanders' favorite beverage. A cup of coffee is a beloved commuting companion or the perfect addition to a catch-up with friends.

SIMPLE. LOCAL. COFFEE.

Map 1; 115 SW Ash Street, Downtown; ///learns.librarian.driver; www.simplelocalcoffeepdx.com

As the name suggests, this comfy coffee shop is all about the local. Owners Lauren and Dave (a barista and a baker) brew their coffee using locally roasted beans, make their chai with a little help from Portland's woman-owned One-Stripe Chai, and create their caramel ciders using housemade caramel sauce. What to enjoy with your drink of choice? One of Dave's seasonal, fruit-filled turnovers should do it.

STUMPTOWN

Map 1; 128 SW 3rd Avenue, Downtown; ///groups.shots.admiral; www.stumptowncoffee.com

Ah, Stumptown: the refuge of tired Downtown office staff popping out for a pick-me-up. The line at this acclaimed coffee shop is often out the door (and not just with besuited professionals). Why? Because

If you're not keen on coffee, make for Smith Tea *(www.smith tea.com)* for beautiful blends of teas.

of Stumptown's long-standing dedication to a) fairly sourcing the world's best beans and b) carefully roasting them to aromatic perfection in-house.

COAVA COFFEE ROASTERS

Map 3; 1300 SE Grand Avenue, Buckman;
///shave.toxic.sober; www.coavacoffee.com

Watch out Stumptown, there's another roaster in town – and it takes its coffee seriously. Not only does Coava ethically source and carefully roast its beans, it also has a rigorous barista training program, so you know your coffee will be good no matter who's making it. Its flagship store – a huge warehouse-style space in Buckman – is often jam-packed with tap-tapping digital nomads and novel-reading creatives.

KOPI COFFEE HOUSE

Map 3; 2327 E Burnside Street, Kerns; ///merit.exchanges.dose;
www.kopicoffeeco.com

This laid-back spot has a huge menu of Southeast Asian drinks. First-timers should try the addictive Indonesian cold brew with cardamom and cream, while the more adventurous can go for the Ube (purple potato) blossom latte. Whatever you choose, you won't regret it.

» **Don't leave without** picking up a bag or two of the coffee shop's whole beans – we love the creamy, caramelly Yunnan Honey.

PORTLAND CÀ PHÊ

Map 5; 2815 SE Holgate Boulevard, Creston-Kenilworth;
///venue.pint.vest; www.portlandcaphe.com

Women-owned café and roasting company Portland Cà Phê is a love-letter to Vietnamese coffee. Sourcing 100 percent of its beans from the Central Highlands of Vietnam, the bright café aims to showcase the versatility of coffee from the country. On the menu is, of course, the famed *cà phê sữa đá* (Vietnamese iced coffee), brewed strong and sweetened with condensed milk (or plant-based milk). But there's so much more to explore: come here for shots of deliciously roasted black coffee and lattes flavored with matcha or cardamom.

RIMSKY-KORSAKOFFEE HOUSE

Map 3; 707 SE 12th Avenue, Buckman; ///minds.dawn.keys; (503) 232-2640

This venerable coffee house only survived the pandemic thanks to a mass community sponsored fundraiser by loyal locals. But they weren't saving the place for its coffee (which is decent, but nothing special). No, they were saving it because Rimsky – with its wacky rotating

Try it!
TAKE A TOUR

Explore Portland's coffee scene with Third Wave Coffee Tours *(www.thirdwavecoffee tours.com)*. You'll sample brews from some of the city's best micro-roasters and cafés, and learn all about coffee making.

and vibrating tables, and spooky, mannequin-filled bathroom – is seen as one of the last remaining relics of so-called "Old Portland." Make like its dedicated fans and come for the eccentric atmosphere, live music performances, and delectable desserts.

NEVER COFFEE

Map 5; 4243 SE Belmont Street, Sunnyside; ///pans.tame.inspector; www.nevercoffeelab.com

Never Coffee is doing things a little differently. Not only is this design-focused coffee shop and roaster eye-catching (we love the jungle-inspired murals), it also offers innovative takes on classic drinks. Sunnysiders can't get enough of its signature beverages, including the warming Hug (made with cocoa, smoked chilies, and cinnamon).

DEADSTOCK

Map 1; 408 NW Couch Street, Old Town/Chinatown; ///cooks.tribes.trials; www.deadstockcoffee.com

One of the few Black-owned coffee shops and roasters in town, Deadstock is the brainchild of Ian Williams, a former shoe designer at Nike. Regulars of this super-cool, sneaker-themed spot have long appreciated it for its neighborly vibe, friendly staff, and incredibly good coffee, including drinks that are hard to find elsewhere. Try the Luther Vandross (aka a silky-smooth lavender mocha) or a Slow Jam (code for the shop's decaf).

» **Don't leave without** devouring one of the bakes Williams' mother, Denise, makes for the shop, like the butterscotch pound cake.

Dive Bars

Adopting a dive bar as your second home is a rite of passage in Portland. Dotted across the city, these dimly lit, shabby spots are usually filled with cheap beer, surly bartenders, and a klatch of disparate regulars.

DOTS CAFE

Map 3; 2521 SE Clinton Street, Richmond; ///minds.lungs.term;
www.dotscafeportland.com

Dots is a tale of two crowds. This diner-esque dive is a homebase for the cantankerous, Rainier-sipping "Old Portland" set, who love ignoring the bar's newer regulars: beanie-topped yuppies who live in the high-end digs that are apparently ruining the neighborhood. It's a fragile harmony fueled by cheap drinks and an eclectic jukebox.

BILLY RAY'S DIVE

Map 4; 2216 NE Martin Luther King Jr. Boulevard, Eliot;
///nests.storms.adjust

By Oregon law, bars serving liquor are required to sell a few hot food items. It's a regulation Billy Ray's mocks by stocking meals that no sober person would ever consume (hello TV dinners) in a freezer below the bar. If this doesn't tell you everything you need to know about this

Billy Ray's is a great place to grab a (cheap) drink before you catch a show at the nearby Wonder Ballroom.

dingy dive bar (seen by many as Portland's best) then pop by for some cheap bottles of Miller High Life and, dare we say, a microwaved meatloaf.

MAD HANNA

Map 6; 6127 NE Fremont Street, Roseway; ///swan.entire.type; www.madhanna.com

A good dive bar should feel like home away from home and for Mad Hanna regulars it's exactly that. Inside this living room-style bar, you can slouch on the comfy couches or challenge your buddies to one of the old-school board games. Outside, the garden has backyard vibes, with locals clustering around the fire pit, playing ping-pong, or knocking back one of the bar's famous jello shots. Nab one yourself (the jiggly cup of lime margarita is the best) and join in the fun.

PAYMASTER LOUNGE

Map 2; 1020 NW 17th Avenue, Pearl District; ///choice.merit.single; www.paymasterlounge.com

This labyrinthine dive is famous for having the best patio west of the Willamette. Grab a seat underneath the massive corrugated roof (warmed by hot-as-hell heat lamps during winter) and kick back with a cheap drink. It's a frequent hangout for post-work 9-to-5-ers and off-duty bartenders, who come here to play pool and blow off steam.
» Don't leave without checking out the eclectic vending machines, which stock everything from retro sweets to fake moustaches.

Solo, Pair, Crowd

Whether you're after a quiet drink or a night out with friends, there's a dive bar for you.

FLYING SOLO
Debate club
Reel 'm Inn's small size makes it a great spot for a solo night out. Settle in with a tallboy and a plate of famed fried chicken and jojos, and strike up a convo with the loyal regulars about whatever is playing on the TV.

IN A PAIR
Conversation starter
The Nest is a classic haunt decorated with kitsch velvet paintings that make for a handy first-date conversation starter. Even better, its ping-pong and pool tables ensure there's no flagging mid-date.

FOR A CROWD
Get the gang together
One of Portland's classier dives, the Art Deco Radio Room is a great place to take your more fastidious friends. Plus, there's a two-story patio, a fire pit, and cushy booths galore.

YAMHILL PUB

Map 1; 223 SW Yamhill Street, Downtown; ///zones.spices.bolt

Like a grease stain on a freshly tailored Armani suit, the Yamhill Pub carries on in brash defiance against its chi-chi capitalist surroundings. Within its graffiti-covered, neon-lit walls, you'll find a surprisingly diverse set of besuited cubicle dwellers, permanent-marker armed pals, and startled out-of-towners who had naively asked their Portland friends to point them in the direction of a truly local hangout. Well, suffice to say, it doesn't get any more local and authentic than a night at this delightfully shambolic bar. As blown-out punk music blares all around you, ignore the craft beers on tap and order a pitcher of Pabst Blue Ribbon – a staple beer of the Yamhill.

SANDY HUT

Map 3; 1430 NE Sandy Boulevard, Buckman; ///spike.march.rushed

For decades, the Sandy Hut was the type of grungy, no-frills place where hardcore drinkers and dejected night shifters downed boilermakers (beer cocktails to the uninitiated). But the march of time – and of development – has since transformed this poorly lit icon into a bit of a hipster hangout. The nicotine-stained walls have been scrubbed (almost) clean and hung with comic book art. Cans of PRB sit next to local craft beers. And the clientele now edges toward freshly tattooed 20-somethings. Despite the spit and polish, old-school regulars and the odd stray biker can't resist popping in for a drink, for old time's sake.

» Don't leave without trying the aptly named Fat Man and Skinny Man – they're two of the best bar burgers in town.

An afternoon in
"Beervana"

With a moniker like "Beervana," it's no surprise that beer reigns supreme in Portland. The first breweries here were set up in the mid-19th century, hot on the heels of the city's founding. Yet it wasn't until the 1980s that craft brewing began to boom, fueled partly by Oregon's impressive hop production and partly by President Carter legalizing home brewing in 1978. Today, the city is home to more breweries, tap houses, and bottle shops than you can shake a stick at, with many of them clustered in and around the Buckman area.

1. Lone Fir Cemetery
649 SE 26th Avenue, Buckman; www.oregonmetro.gov
///farms.prime.pine

2. Cascade
939 SE Belmont Street, Buckman; www.cascade brewingbarrelhouse.com
///star.medium.cherry

3. Loyal Legion
710 SE 6th Avenue, Buckman; www.loyallegionpdx.com
///double.pigs.estate

4. Wayfinder Beer
304 SE 2nd Avenue, Buckman; www.wayfinder.beer
///rounds.swaps.opera

📍 **Oregon Brewers Festival** ///outer.shirts.vanish

Steel Bridge

OLD TOWN

WEST BURNSIDE ST

*Taking place in Tom McCall Waterfront Park, the **Oregon Brewers Festival** is one of the best craft beer festivals in the world.*

Hawthorne Bridge

Marquam Bridge

**Finish up at
WAYFINDER BEER**

Head over to this
award-winning brewery
to devour a huge plate of
nachos, washed down
with one of its famously
refreshing lagers.

**Start your beer
pilgrimage at
LONE FIR
CEMETERY**

This leafy spot is home
to the tomb of George
Frederic Bottler who,
along with his brother
George Michael Bottler,
founded some of the first
breweries in Oregon.

**Get sampling at
LOYAL LEGION**

Take a tour of Oregon's
brewing scene at this tap
house, which is home
to almost 100 beers and
ciders on tap – all made
in Oregon, of course.

**Drop by
CASCADE**

Pick up a few bottles of
funky sour beer from this
offbeat brewery to enjoy
later; it was a pioneer
of the Pacific Northwest's
sour brews movement.

KERNS

NORTHEAST

Buckman
Field

SANDY BOULEVARD

BANFIELD FREEWAY

I-5

NORTHEAST

EAST BURNSIDE STREET

BUCKMAN

SOUTHEAST STARK ST

SOUTHEAST MORRISON STREET

SE ALDER STREET

Colonel
Summers
Park

SOUTHEAST HAWTHORNE BOULEVARD

SOUTHEAST

HOSFORD
ABERNETHY

LADD'S
ADDITION

0 meters 500
0 yards 500

SHOP

Forget generic stores and the usual buys: Portlanders love to thrift for one-of-a-kind clothes, pick up vinyl from local record labels, and get nerdy with comics and games.

Comics and Games

Jam-packed with comic book shops and games stores, Portland is the perfect place to get your nerd on. Most stores offer events too, from graphic novel reading clubs to Dungeons & Dragons tournaments.

RED CASTLE GAMES

Map 5; 7160 SE Foster Road, Foster-Powell; ///traps.jumps.weeks; www.redcastlegames.com

Planning a weekend of battling orcs and casting spells? Red Castle Games has you covered. This store is jam-packed with RPG (role-playing games to the uninitiated) and collectible card games, including everyone's favorite, Magic: The Gathering. Role-playing veterans descend on the store for nail-biting tournaments, while newbies pick up the essentials for an at-home games night with the roomies.

FLOATING WORLD COMICS

Map 1; 400 NW Couch Street, Old Town/Chinatown; ///zest.across.could; www.floatingworldcomics.com

Famous superhero comics are definitely not the name of the game at this cliché-defying store. Instead, it celebrates the underdogs of the comic book world, specializing in small press and underground offerings; it even publishes its own comics and graphic novels. Come to pick up a new release by local publishers like Dark Horse or grab a unique read from a budding artist. Oh, and there's the chance to attend talks and book launches on the regular, too.

GUARDIAN GAMES

Map 3; 345 SE Taylor Street, Buckman;
///analogy.scans.dust; www.ggportland.com

Gone are the days when you'd keep your Dungeons & Dragons addiction secret. Today, board games are undeniably mainstream – and Guardian Games knows it. Portlanders of all stripes come to browse the shelves at this warehouse-sized store, before sitting down at one of the communal tables to do battle with their friends. Grab a beer from the bar in the back and go join in the fun.

» Don't leave without booking in for one of the store's famous Magic: The Gathering tournaments (Monday and Friday evenings).

Woman-owned Books With Pictures *(www.bookswith pictures.com)* is still under the radar – but don't expect it to stay that way for long. This cute shop is all about inclusivity, focusing on comics and stories with diverse representation, whether that's with regards to sexual orientation, disability, gender expression, race, or age. Even better, they also offer community events, including a comic book club.

Liked by the locals

"Bridge City Comics hosts great comic book release and signing parties for local comic creators. Also, their subscription packages are an excellent introduction for people interested in comics but not sure where to start."

CASSANDRA CARTER, LOCAL ARTIST, MUSICIAN, AND COMICS ENTHUSIAST

BRIDGE CITY COMICS

Map 4; 3725 N Mississippi Avenue, Boise; ///obey.tame.worker; www.bridgecitycomics.com

Bridge City has all the vibes of a community bookshop. Here, an eclectic mix of comic book fans (from hoodie-clad high school kids to moustachioed hipsters) peruse the wooden shelves, occasionally asking the friendly staff for advice. The store also hosts a chilled reading club for fans of graphic novels (every second Thursday of the month).

CLOUD CAP GAMES

Map 6; 1226 SE Lexington Street, Sellwood-Moreland; ///both.alert.custom; https://cloudcapgames.com

Sellwood locals adore this little shop, which was set up by Kirsten and James Brady to spread their love of board games. It's basically a big kid's den with its patterned rugs, fairy-tale tree (made from scrap wood), and, of course, stacks upon stacks of colorful table-top games.
» Don't leave without trying before you buy. Pay $5 to rent any game for three nights; even better, the fee gets deducted if you do buy.

KINOKUNIYA PORTLAND

Map 1; 829 SW 9th Avenue, Downtown; ///tags.sticks.angle; https://usa.kinokuniya.com

Japanophiles can lose days in Kinokuniya. A mash-up of a bookstore and art shop, this light, airy spot is packed with Japanese comics, toys, and more. Here, hardcore manga-fans browse the huge collection of graphic novels, while teenagers pick up packets of Pokémon cards.

Home Touches

*Apartment dressing in Portland is all about creativity
and individuality. As long as it's characterful, made
with love, and, most importantly, won't be found in
a friend's house, Portlanders are all for it.*

ROOTS & CROWNS

**Map 2; 1812 NW 24th Avenue, Slabtown; ///prom.gifts.across;
www.rootsandcrowns.com**

This queer-owned apothecary is all about self care. Inspired by the
healing power of plants, owner Max Turk whips up a magical range
of herbal products, such as natural perfumes and soothing tinctures.
Join work-weary Portlanders stocking up on relaxing goodies, and
remember to grab one of Turk's signature essential oil blends, too —
it'll have your home smelling lovely in the blink of an eye.

CARGO

**Map 3; 81 SE Yamhill Street, Central Eastside;
///worker.fields.quiz; www.cargoinc.com**

Cargo is like a multicolored treasure trove on steroids. The huge
warehouse space is bursting at the seams with unique, handmade
objects sourced from makers and artists around the globe. Want to

stock up on cute handpainted mugs? No problem. Hunting for Indian torans? Cargo can help. Looking for a painted table from Indonesia? Come on, you know the answer.

>> Don't leave without treating yourself to some of the gorgeous handmade jewelry; the Indian necklaces are stunning.

PISTILS NURSERY

Map 4; 3811 N Mississippi Avenue, Boise;
///trace.spring.cafe; www.pistilsnursery.com

The only thing more millennial than having countless houseplants is somehow managing to kill them every few months (or, let's be honest, weeks). Thankfully, there's Pistils. This urban jungle is filled with more plants than you could feasibly dispatch in a lifetime: fronds of foliage blanket the floor, succulents and cacti jostle for room on the rustic shelves, and leafy plants dangle from the ceiling. Dodge the other eager plant parents and pick up a requisite cheese plant or show-stopping parlor palm. Just remember to water it this time.

Try it!
GET GARDENING

Book on to a Houseplants 101 workshop at Pistils Nursery to unearth precisely what your plant babies need. The nursery runs loads of other classes, too, like plant propagation and *kokedama* making.

Solo, Pair, Crowd

Shopping for your apartment? Hunting for bargains with your pals? Portland's got something for every spending spree.

FLYING SOLO
Pick up a bargain
The Reclaimory specializes in restoring vintage home goods, with some killer deals on beautiful mid-century furniture. Go alone, or you'll be fighting with your buddy over that teak coffee table.

IN A PAIR
DIY goodies
Need supplies for that DIY project that you and your other half have been meaning to do? Make for Hippo Hardware. An icon for decades on East Burnside, it sells a massive collection of eclectic household hardware.

FOR A CROWD
Head to market
Friends love visiting the Portland Night Market, as there's something to suit everyone's taste. Here, hundreds of stalls sell an eclectic variety of locally made goods, from incense to terrariums.

TENDER LOVING EMPIRE
Map 5; 412 SW 10th Avenue, Downtown;
///poster.stews.grows; www.tenderlovingempire.com

If you're looking to take home a slice of the city, head to Tender Loving Empire. A bastion of Portland-made items, its bright stores (including its flagship in Downtown) are filled on the weekends with artsy types looking to find handcrafted mugs and colorful art prints.

» Don't leave without picking up one of the vinyls produced by TLE's record label, including offerings by Portland-based musicians.

PAXTON GATE
Map 4; 4204 N Mississippi Avenue, Boise;
///films.brass.deed; www.paxtongate.com

There are no soy candles or handcrafted vases at Paxton Gate – oh no, this place is full-on "Portland weird." Taxidermied animal heads dot the walls, while pinned insects, glittering crystals, and human skulls (no jokes) line the shelves. Portlanders come here to grab a gift for that friend who has everything – apart from a bat skeleton, of course.

SHE BOP
Map 5; 3213 SE Division Street, Richmond;
///glare.reader.caged; www.sheboptheshop.com

This women-owned, super-inclusive sex-toy boutique sells all the bedroom essentials you could ever need (think vibrators, plugs, and gender expression implements). It's wonderfully sex positive, too, hosting events on things like sex parties and exploring gender identity.

Book Nooks

Portlanders bypass characterless corporates for charming independents, where arty volumes, philosophical tomes, and social-justice books feed their topical interests.

WALLACE BOOKS

Map 6; 7241 SE Milwaukie Avenue, Sellwood-Moreland; ///paying.formed.storms; (503) 235-7350

Step inside this sweet 1930s wooden house and you'll feel like you're inside the library of an eccentric professor. Books are every which way you turn, stacked from floor to ceiling and spilling out of crates and boxes. Not just dog-eared classics, mind — delicious new releases lie in wait, too. You'll need a good few hours to delve through the mounds of books, and a tote to ferry your newly purchased treasures home.

POWELL'S BOOKS

Map 1; 1005 W Burnside Street, Pearl District; ///ballots.future.quiz; www.powells.com

Let's be real: we couldn't have a list of Portland bookstores and not mention the icon that is Powell's. Known as a "City of Books," this colossus takes up an entire square block and houses hundreds of thousands of tomes. Among its maze of shelves, self-professed thinkers flick through works by Kant and Proust, and students pick up stacks of used books. After a first edition? Head to the Rare Book Room, but be warned: you'll need sharp elbows to fight off the other collectors.

» Don't leave without sipping on a latte in the café, where you can watch the bustle on West Burnside Street through huge windows.

BROADWAY BOOKS

Map 4; 1714 NE Broadway, Sullivan's Gulch;
///ends.point.shell; www.broadwaybooks.net

Sure, Powell's is the big shot in town, but it can't beat Broadway for its friendly neighborhood feel. Set up in 1992 by Gloria Olds and Roberta Dyer, two friends with an insatiable passion for books, this cute store is known for its impressive selection of titles and chatty staff, who know pretty much everything there is to know about books. Plus, it regularly hosts events by emerging and established writers; Michelle Obama once did a talk here – enough said.

DAEDALUS BOOKS

Map 2; 2074 NW Flanders Street, Nob Hill;
///latter.gravel.woes; (503) 274-7742

Focusing on art, philosophy, and music, this unassuming secondhand store is tilled with all the books you didn't know you needed. Gloriously random finds might include a book on tattoo art or a collection of poems about Elvis. Whatever you pick up here, it's certain to make a great conversation starter next time your friends pop round.

GREEN BEAN BOOKS

Map 4; 1600 NE Alberta, Alberta Arts District;
///items.clown.thick; www.greenbeanbookspdx.com

After a birthday present for your niece or nephew? Make for Green Bean. Beloved by families, this cozy kids' bookstore is bursting with quirky toys, squashy armchairs, and – you guessed it – row upon row of wonderful books. There are plenty of the usual classics tucked onto the shelves, but you'll also find inclusive and social justice-themed stories here, too.

ANNIE BLOOM'S BOOKS

Map 6; 7834 SW Capitol Highway, Multnomah Village;
///form.level.goods; www.annieblooms.com

It's little wonder Annie Bloom's is a longtime favorite of Multnomah Village residents. Not only does this bookshop offer a broad range of new books (the handpicked fiction titles are a highlight) and

Shh!

Buckman locals want to keep Mother Foucault's Bookshop (*www.motherfoucaultsbookshop. com*) firmly under their hats. Why? Because they don't want to have to share its excellent collection of used, rare, and vintage books with anyone. Dare their wrath by browsing the book-strewn shelves at this charming spot, or attend one of the store's evening book readings or launches, which take place Thursday to Sunday.

top-notch customer service (the staff are avid readers), it also hosts author events, such as book signings and live readings. Best of all, it's home to a resident black cat named Mollie Bloom, who can often be found asleep in her basket by the cash register. Cute, right?

THIRD EYE BOOKS, ACCESSORIES & GIFTS
Map 5; 2518 SE 33rd Avenue, Richmond;
///means.vibrates.many; www.thirdeyebag.com

Back in 2019, Charles Hannah and Michelle Lewis launched Third Eye from their kitchen table. Fast-forward a few years and, with the help of a fundraiser, this bookshop is now happily settled in the trendy Richmond neighborhood. Its shelves are packed with titles that are inclusive, social-justice themed, and – unlike many bookstores in town – specifically serve the city's Black readers.

NEW RENAISSANCE BOOKSHOP
Map 2; 1338 NW 23rd Avenue, Nob Hill;
///senior.pizza.nature; www.newrenbooks.com

The suburbia-style exterior of New Renaissance Bookshop is utterly misleading. Why? Because visiting this New Age spot is like stepping into a hippie wonderland. Serenaded by the peals of windchimes, laid-back Nob Hill locals leisurely leaf through the selection of mystical books on offer, which cover everything from astrology to crystals.

» **Don't leave without** checking out some of the classes on offer, including meditation sessions and astrological predictions.

Record Stores

Portland is heaven on earth for curious crate diggers with time and money to burn. Join rockers and jazz lovers between aisles of old and new vinyl, as you keep an eye out for elusive albums.

CROSSROADS MUSIC

Map 5; 8112 SE Harold Street, Foster-Powell;
///tricky.marked.take; www.xro.com

Welcome to the city's biggest and best selection of used vinyl: jazz, krautrock, post-punk, funk – you name it, Crossroads has it. Browsing can be a time-consuming business, though, as over 35 different vendors sell their finds here, and each has their own, let's say idiosyncratic, system of organization. Block out an afternoon for rummaging and get ready to unearth some rare, out-there vinyl.

JACKPOT RECORDS

Map 5; 3574 SE Hawthorne Boulevard, Hawthorne;
///admits.relate.scar; www.jackpotrecords.com

Nestled among the vintage shops of the hippie Hawthorne neighborhood, this iconic record store attracts discerning musos old and young with its flawlessly curated collection. Beneath a neon

All that crate digging left you hungry? Make for nearby Farmhouse Kitchen to refuel on tasty Thai street food.

pink "Records" sign, you'll find every genre from hip-hop to metal, but the best thing is the eclectic range of vinyl produced by the store's own record label.

MISSISSIPPI RECORDS

Map 4; 5202 N Albina Avenue, Humboldt;
///bless.stick.simple; www.mississippirecords.net

This spot casts off the whole grungy, dusty record store feel in favor of a more laid-back look: think hardwood floors, globe lights, and the occasional potted plant. In fact, it feels more like a studio apartment from a trendy design magazine than a record store. But vinyl there is, mainly a carefully curated collection of soul, blues, funk, jazz, and rock. Want to broaden your horizons? Check out the rack of albums released by Mississippi's own in-house label (near the cash register).

>> Don't leave without peeking at the vintage stereo repair shop out back, which sometimes sells restored turntables, receivers, and the like.

LITTLE AXE RECORDS

Map 4; 4122 NE Sandy Boulevard, Hollywood;
///crisp.sculpture.invent; www.littleaxerecords.com

Little Axe is the place to expand your musical horizons. Come the weekend, this cute shop is full of inquisitive music lovers checking out the eclectic range of little-known artists and genres from around the world (think Burmese harp music and Tuareg desert blues). Plus, the store has a huge collection of cassette tapes – yes, they're back.

VINYL RESTING PLACE
Map 6; 8332 N Lombard Street, St Johns;
///pressuring.believer.commenced; www.vinylrestingplaceusa.com

Tucked away in the leafy St. Johns neighborhood, this little record store has more going for it than just a fantastically puntastic name. Jazz and blues lovers from across town head to this snug space to pick up everything from new vinyl releases to obscure classics. Blues and jazz not your jam? They have a great assortment of classic rock, punk, and folk, too. Vinyl also hosts two $1 record sales during the year; one after the annual St. Johns Parade in May, and the other in September, to celebrate the store's birthday.

MUSIC MILLENNIUM
Map 5; 3158 E Burnside Street, Laurelhurst;
///best.indeed.drama; www.musicmillennium.com

It's not possible to have a list of Portland record stores and miss out Music Millennium. After all, this legendary spot is the city's oldest record store. It's still going strong today, largely thanks to its fiercely independent owner, Terry Currier, whose knowledge of music verges on the encyclopedic. (FYI, he was the one who coined the "Keep Portland Weird" slogan, as a way to champion the city's indie businesses.) The multistory space is often packed with roving crate diggers, touring musicians, and music-obsessed out-of-towners, who pilgrimage here to pour over the well-curated, genre-diverse vinyl collection.

» Don't leave without making plans to come back for one of the in-store performances by an up-and-coming act.

Liked by the locals

"Portland has such a strong record store scene because everyone here has to be at the top of their game – we all try to get the coolest inventory, which makes for a creative culture. Plus, it rains a lot here, so hanging indoors and playing records is a big, big deal."

TERRY CURRIER, OWNER OF MUSIC MILLENNIUM

Vintage Gems

Not ones to follow the crowd, Portlanders are all about thrifting for one-of-a-kind clothes. Hawthorne is the city's secondhand hub (p112), but there are plenty more vintage stores beyond this bohemian neighborhood.

MAGPIE VINTAGE

Map 3; 1960 SE Hawthorne Boulevard, Hawthorne; ///trucks.labels.unique; (503) 946-1153

Ah, Magpie — there's always a surprise hidden in your nest. Beady-eyed Portlanders descend on this charming store, which bursts with vintage finds from the 1890s through to the 1990s, to hunt for unusual threads. Browse the racks to find things like a 1930s sequinned bolero jacket (perfect for a friend's birthday) or Edwardian-era Oxfords (to elevate your office outfit game).

RED LIGHT CLOTHING EXCHANGE

Map 5; 3590 SE Hawthorne Boulevard, Hawthorne; ///offer.empire.shiny; www.shopredlight.com

The closet of an 80s fashionista — that's what Red Light brings to mind. The rails here are rammed with retro bell-bottomed jeans, colorful jumpsuits, and MC Hammer-style pants (plus a few items

Visit during the week: you'll have the racks (almost) to yourself and are more likely to grab a good find. | from other eras). On weekends, the store is swamped with teenagers on the hunt for poofy prom dresses, or partygoers keen for uber-retro leopard-print tops.

ARTIFACT: CREATIVE RECYCLE

Map 5; 3630 SE Division Street, Richmond;
///same.cuts.butter; www.artifactpdx.com

This secondhand clothing store sells a super-cool collection of modern and vintage apparel (think ripped jeans, colorful berets, and embroidered jackets). Sure, there's heaps of style, but there's also a ton of substance: eco-warrior owner Leah Meijer wants to reduce the impact on the planet by encouraging folks to buy pre-loved items, via both the store and a summer flea market.

» **Don't leave without** shopping in the back staging room, where Artifact keeps its carefully selected antique furniture and decor.

RED FOX VINTAGE

Map 5; 4528 SE Woodstock Boulevard, Woodstock;
///become.radar.cheek; (971) 302-7065

Woodstock locals adore this funky shop, which stocks every vintage item under the sun. Here, couples shop for antique furniture, while crate diggers flick through boxes of vinyl. There's even a "man cave" at the back, filled with everything from well-loved Levi's to beer steins. Don't forget to pick up a flannel shirt while you're here – it's the unofficial uniform of the Pacific Northwest.

HOUSE OF VINTAGE

Map 5; 3315 SE Hawthorne Boulevard, Hawthorne;
///hype.beams.sugar; www.houseofvintagenw.com/portland

Don't be fooled: this isn't a house of vintage, it's a mansion. The huge space is home to over 60 vendors, selling all kinds of secondhand bits and bobs. After an 80s track jacket? You got it. On the hunt for cowboy boots? Take your pick. Retro garms aside, there's everything from pre-loved furniture to (ahem) vintage *Playboy* magazines.

WORKSHOP VINTAGE

Map 4; 4011 N Williams Avenue, Williams;
///puppy.always.healthier; www.workshopvintage.com

Audra Santillo and Nate Moore take vintage seriously, roaming the Pacific Northwest to unearth upscale gems. Each and every stylish find makes its way to their store, which is frequented by elegant

Tucked away in Sellwood-Moorland is Old Portland Hardware & Architectural *(www.oldportlandhardware. com)*, a massive warehouse-style space jam-packed with funky vintage finds. Design-minded locals come here to get stuff for their apartments, whether it's an industrial-style lamp or a piece of jewel-bright stained glass. Even better, the store sells unique originals made from otherwise unwanted items, like Singer Sewing Machine tables.

Williams locals in search of designer gear. Workshop isn't just about secondhand finery, though. Items by local artisans also dot the shelves (we heart the quirky jewelry), as do the owners' own labors of love: Audra crafts the store's leather goods, while Nate, a woodworker, creates shelves, tables, and more. What a talented duo.

BANSHEE

Map 3; 2410 E Burnside Street, Buckman; ///shack.level.paint; www.shopbanshee.com

Banshee is less typical vintage store and more upscale boutique, thanks to a minimalist white interior and color-coded rails. Chic girlfriends heart this spot for the well-curated vintage clothes; all the items here are in great shape and have been picked with modern trends in mind, so while they are vintage, they don't feel like it.

» Don't leave without checking out the store's artisan-made homewares, including cute pottery pieces and small-batch skincare.

HOLLYWOOD VINTAGE

Map 4; 2757 Northeast Pacific Street, Kerns; ///lamp.damage.pages; (503) 233-1890

Cash-strapped students direct their steps to Hollywood Vintage whenever a fancy dress party is on the cards. They comb the rails of this giant warehouse, where garish clown pants and 1920s fedoras sit alongside Clark Kent-style glasses and Cruella de Vil-esque fur coats. It's all good quality, too, so you can hold on to that vintage smoking jacket long after you stop pretending to be Sherlock Holmes.

Portland Made

Nonbinary clothing, handmade cannabis pipes, and carefully crafted candles: Portland's design scene is a force to be reckoned with. Stop by one of these super-cool stores to take home a slice of the city.

BETSY AND IYA

Map 2; 1777 NW 24th Avenue, Slabtown;
///agree.noses.cheat; www.betsyandiya.com

When Portlanders are hunting for unique jewelry, they turn to this cute little store, where bold, geometric designs rule. Everything is expertly handmade, with most of the items dreamt up by co-owner Betsy Cross and crafted locally (right in the studio next door, in fact). They're the kind of pieces you'd spot on your most stylish friend, so be quick and grab those Art Deco-style earrings before they do.

WILDFANG

Map 1; 404 SW 10th Avenue, Downtown;
///acting.range.stands; www.wildfang.com

Super-cool Wildfang has been challenging gender norms since its inception. Co-founders Emma McIlroy and Julia Parsley were tired of men's clothes being just "for the boys," so they began designing menswear for women and nonbinary people: think blazers with real pockets and button-ups without boob gaps. If that wasn't awesome enough, the pair make sure their clothes are sustainably and ethically made, as well as donating money to progressive causes like ACLU and Planned Parenthood.

» **Don't leave without** grabbing a couple of the store's famous "Wild Feminist" tees for you and your buddies.

LADIES OF PARADISE
Map 2; 1500 NW 18th Avenue, Suite 111, Slabtown;
///afford.tells.clock; www.ladiesofparadise.com

This women-owned boutique is all about celebrating Portland's legal and socially acceptable weed culture. Alongside stylish boxes of cannabis, you'll find plenty of weed-centric accessories – all from female artists and brands, naturally. Here, super-stylish girlfriends browse for brightly colored stash jars, cute necklaces that hold roach clips, and geometric pipes . Our favorites are the funky tees, especially the UFO-themed "Higher than a spaceship."

Try it!
CANNABIS CULTURE

Looking to try cannabis? Head to the Green Muse (www.gogreenmuse.com). This Black-owned pot dispensary is known for its top-notch cannabis flowers, including the wildly popular Runtz.

Liked by the locals

"Portland Saturday Market is pretty amazing. Everybody selling at the market is an artist and everything is handmade. Then there's the culture of being at the market: the energetic vibe and being with other artists is unreal."

TOBIN FLOOM, A PHOTOGRAPHER AND ONE OF THE
VENDORS AT THE PORTLAND SATURDAY MARKET

MADEHERE

Map 1; 40 NW 10th Avenue, Pearl District;
///slap.plus.mouse; www.madehereonline.com

MadeHere is a kind of heaven for fashionable Portlanders. Not only are all the goods design-focused, they're also housed in a beautiful gallery-style space that makes browsing a joy. Come here to pick up things like handmade leather wallets and spruce-spiked wax candles.

PORTLAND SATURDAY MARKET

Map 1; 2 SW Naito Parkway, Downtown; ///trying.data.picked;
www.portlandsaturdaymarket.com

This open-air market has the vibe of a street party: buskers strum away at their guitars, street performers careen around on stilts, and the aroma of delicious baked goods fills the air. And the stalls themselves? Expect an excess of locally made goodies, of course, like handcrafted ceramics and chopping boards fashioned out of reclaimed wood.

>> Don't leave without hitting up Bonus Pants, a stall selling comedy undies, including the planets-decorated "Uranus."

SCAPEGOAT TATTOO

Map 3; 1233 SE Stark Street, Buckman; ///opera.modern.inch;
www.scapegoattattoo.com

It's true: Portland is one of the most inked-up cities in the US. So what better reminder of its creative culture than getting a tattoo? Vegan-friendly Scapegoat can sort you out. Here, join sleeve-toting hipsters getting tatted up by seasoned artists – how about a Portland rose?

A morning of vintage shopping in
Hawthorne

Portland is up there when it comes to vintage shopping in the US. This is a city that's big on self-expression, with locals preferring to style themselves and their homes in unique secondhand pieces, rather than anything mass-produced. And if Portland is a vintage hub, then Hawthorne is its heart. Come the weekend, thrifty locals on the hunt for kooky threads and antique furniture head to this haute-hippie wonderland to spend hours rummaging through its countless vintage stores.

1. Red Light Clothing Exchange
3590 SE Hawthorne Boulevard, Hawthorne;
www.shopredlight.com
///offer.empire.shiny

2. House of Vintage
3315 SE Hawthorne Boulevard, Hawthorne;
www.houseofvintagenw.com
///hype.beams.sugar

📍 **Fred's Sound of Music**
///strut.claps.outer

3. Tov
207 SE Hawthorne Boulevard, Hawthorne;
www.tovcoffee.com
///crazy.fantastic.appear

4. Vintage Pink
2500 SE Hawthorne Boulevard, Hawthorne;
www.ilovevintagepink.com
///crown.deeply.spot

5. National Hat Museum
1928 SE Ladd Avenue, Ladd's Addition; www.thehatmuseum.com
///ozone.others.open

BUCKMAN

SOUTHEAST

Colonel Summers Park

20TH AVENUE

SE HAWTHORNE BOULEVARD

LADD'S ADDITION

SOUTHEAST ELLIOTT AVENUE

5

End your morning at the NATIONAL HAT MUSEUM
Admire head toppers throughout the ages at this quirky museum, which is filled with over 2,000 different hats, from Victorian to modern.

HOSFORD-ABERNETHY

Laurelhurst
Park

SOUTHEAST CÉSAR E. CHAVEZ BLVD

SOUTHEAST STARK STREET

Lone Fir
Cemetery

SOUTHEAST

SOUTHEAST 26TH AVENUE

SUNNYSIDE

SOUTHEAST BELMONT STREET

Refuel at
TOV

Grab a take-out
Egyptian-style coffee at
this café housed inside
an old double-decker
bus, then take a stroll
around nearby
Seawallcrest Park.

Pop into
RED LIGHT
CLOTHING
EXCHANGE

Rake through the rails at this
local institution. It has a
massive collection of vintage
clothes, including a huge
number of epic 80s outfits.

4 SE HAWTHORNE BOULEVARD **3** **2** **1**

HAWTHORNE

Style your home at
VINTAGE PINK

Browse the vintage home
decor and furniture at this
funky emporium, easily
recognizable by its bright-
pink exterior. It can be a
bit pricey – but that stylish
mid-century clock will look
great in your apartment.

Get lost in
HOUSE OF
VINTAGE

Spend some time
wandering through this
huge store, home to all
kinds of vintage items,
including retro vinyl,
old-school artworks,
and countless clothes.

SOUTHEAST 24TH AVENUE

SOUTHEAST 34TH AVENUE

Opened in 1948, **Fred's
Sound of Music** *is one
of the oldest electronic
stores in the US. Today,
it sells and repairs
vintage stereos.*

SOUTHEAST DIVISION STREET

RICHMOND

| 0 meters | 400 |
| 0 yards | 400 |

ARTS & CULTURE

It's fair to say, Portland's creative scene is pretty kooky (no surprises there). Art bursts with social commentary, while quirky collections tickle the imagination.

City History

From Native American settlement to major hippie hangout and beyond, Portland sure has a rich history. The city has a dark past of discrimination, too, a legacy that it continues to struggle with.

NICHAQWLI MONUMENT

Map 6; 21224 NE Blue Lake Road, Fairview; ///devise.because.furious; www.oregonmetro.gov/parks/blue-lake-regional-park

Overlooking tranquil Blue Lake, this replica of a traditional village celebrates the heritage of the region's Native American Nichaqwli people. Carved cedar house posts and a basalt net sinker give you an idea of what the village would have looked like in days gone by, while an interpretive sign tells the story of the villagers.

MCMENAMINS CRYSTAL BALLROOM

Map 1; 1332 W Burnside Street, Downtown; ///trend.volunteered.gosh; www.crystalballroompdx.com

Back in the 1960s, this iconic music venue *(p154)* was a hotbed for hippie activity. Psychedelic rock bands like the Grateful Dead and The Electric Prunes performed here, surrounded by tie-dye wearing Portlanders who bounced about on the Crystal's "floating" dance

Take a tour of the 100-year-old Crystal Ballroom to learn more about its past *(www. mcmenamins.com)*.

floor. Okay, there aren't many long-haired bohemians knocking around today, but this spot is still one of the best places in Portland to rock out.

SHANGHAI TUNNELS

Map 1; 226 NW Davis Street, Old Town/Chinatown;
///spit.hogs.couches; www.otbrewing.com

Lurking under the streets of Old Town/Chinatown is a hidden network of legendary tunnels, built in the 19th century when the city was a busy maritime hub. Some claim these subterranean paths were used by sailors to reach opium dens and brothels; others that they housed kidnapped sailors, a practice known as "Shanghaiing." (The evidence for either is pretty slim, but we can't deny they make for a good story.) If you fancy taking a look, Old Town Brewing offers one-hour tours of its (reputedly haunted) section of the tunnels.

PITTOCK MANSION

Map 2; 3229 NW Pittock Drive, Forest Park; ///sock.global.dine;
www.pittockmansion.org

Found in leafy Forest Park, this stately mansion was built in 1914 by publishing magnate Henry Pittock. Join out-of-towners and school groups as they wander through its historic rooms, admiring the period furniture and family heirlooms, including a masonic sword.
» Don't leave without taking in the epic view of Portland from behind the mansion; you can even spy Mount Hood in the distance.

PORTLAND CHINATOWN MUSEUM
Map 1; 127 NW 3rd Avenue, Old Town/Chinatown;
///fried.social.admiral; www.portlandchinatownmuseum.org
In the late 19th century, Portland was home to the second-largest Chinatown on the West Coast. While the neighborhood may no longer be the hub of Portland's Chinese American community, the area's heritage is still celebrated today – especially at this excellent museum. It tells the stories of the Chinese immigrants who helped build the city, and hosts great rotating exhibits, too.

VANPORT HISTORICAL MARKER
Map 6; 1809 N Broadacre Road, Delta Park; ///snack.bumpy.spaces
Today, Portland is seen as liberal and progressive, but this wasn't always the case. In fact, the city has a long history of discrimination and racism, especially against Black communities. Nowhere is this

Shh!

Glance down at the sidewalk when strolling around the city and you might just spy a horse ring. Dating from the 19th century, when horses were the main means of transportation, these metal hoops were used to tether your noble steed. In true kooky Portland style, there's now a "Horse Project," where tiny toy miniatures of the real thing are tied to the rings. Visit the Woodstock neighborhood, birthplace of the project, for your best chance of seeing some.

more poignantly seen than at Vanport. Set up in 1942 for migrant shipyard workers, this makeshift city quickly became a de facto ghetto for African American workers (segregationist housing policies barred them from living in Portland proper). Tragedy struck in the spring of 1948, when the Columbia River rose over 20 in (50 cm) and the marshy area that housed Vanport was flooded, displacing nearly 20,000 residents. All that remains now is an empty grassy space, home to a plaque that commemorates the thousands of its residents (over 6,000 of whom were Black) who were left without a home. It's a stark reminder of Portland's troubled recent history.

>> Don't leave without visiting the Black Pacific Northwest Collection a couple of miles south of Vanport. It preserves and celebrates the history of the Black experience in the area via books, records, and films.

OREGON HISTORICAL SOCIETY
Map 1; 1200 SW Park Avenue, Downtown;
///slate.assure.frog; www.ohs.org

This interactive museum is a wild ride through Oregon's rich and complicated past. Exhibits here cover everything from the history of the area's Indigenous peoples and the heritage of Portland's Japanese immigrants to the exploration of the coast and the evolution of mountain sports. The busiest display, though, is without a doubt Portland's famous penny (bear with us). It's said that, in 1845, the city's co-founders (Asa Lovejoy of Boston, Massachusetts, and Francis Pettygrove of Portland, Maine) decided the name of the booming settlement by flipping this penny. Suffice to say that Francis had all the luck that day.

Street Art

Often acting as historical records or serving up social commentary, Portland's murals are about so much more than adding a splash of color to the city streets – although they do this in spades, too.

ART FILLS THE VOID

Map 3; 1125 SE Division Street, Hosford-Abernethy; ///manual.arts.spell

Back in the early 80s, the puntastically named Gorilla Wallflare – a collective of anonymous graffiti artists – waged war on the city's drab walls. One of their best-known pieces is a mural of a banana with the slogan "Art fills the void" next to it – a nod to the idea that these blank walls were nothing but unrealized potential. Today, this iconic mural is one of the oldest pieces of street art in the city.

WOMEN MAKING HISTORY IN PORTLAND

Map 4; 2399 N Harding Avenue, Eliot; ///purely.nods.press

Girl power is on big, bold, and bright display at this mural on the edge of Interstate Avenue. It depicts over a dozen influential women who called Portland home at one point, like the affordable housing advocate Susan Emmons and youth outreach activist Antoinette Edwards.

KEEP PORTLAND WEIRD

Map 1; 350 W Burnside Street, Old Town/Chinatown; ///edits.master.worm

When Music Millennium *(p102)* owner Terry Currier coined the "Keep Portland Weird" slogan, he didn't expect it to become the city's unofficial motto. But the phrase resonated – so much so that it's become part of the fabric of Portland. It now pops up across the city, including this huge mural behind debauched punk bar Dante's *(p159)*.

» Don't leave without checking out the mini version of this mural – found on the side of the Music Millennium building, of course.

ATTITUDE OF GRATITUDE

Map 3; 959 SE Division Street, Hosford-Abernethy; ///quit.trunk.older

Soaring 70 ft (21 m) high, this staggering mural shows a woman standing in a grateful pose, hands together as if in prayer. Yeah it's huge, but its size isn't the most remarkable thing about it. No, what really catches everyone's eye is the figure's hair, which is made up of over 1,000 lush, tumbling – and completely real – plants.

Try it!
TAKE AN ARTY TOUR

Portland Street Art Alliance offers tours of the city's murals, touching on their history, active community art projects (some of which they help fund), and the politics of public space *(www.pdxstreetart.org)*.

Liked by the locals

"Street art offers imagery to stir up positive thoughts. When a new mural or piece of street art or graffiti goes up, it offers a chance for discovery, some new colors to experience, and a sense of novelty that can have a stimulating effect on the viewer's state of mind."

RATHER SEVERE, STREET ARTIST DUO

BLACK UNITED FUND BUILDING

Map 4; 2828 NE Alberta Street, Alberta Arts District; ///clear.sunk.letter

Once the heart of Portland's Black community, Alberta has been subject to sweeping gentrification. Despite this, though, efforts are being made to preserve its heritage *(p136)*. A striking example is the empowering mural on the side of this community-focused building, featuring acclaimed Black women, such as activist Angela Davis.

OUT OF THE SHADE

Map 1; 404-418 SW 2nd Avenue, Downtown; ///soaks.brave.precautions

In December 2016, Blaine Fontana, one of Portland's most famous muralists and a survivor of depression, braved the cold winter weather to paint this massive, colorful mural. Emblazoned with a bird and the words "Out of the Shade," the piece encourages people to talk about depression and provides a message of hope.

» Don't leave without visiting vibrant mural "I Gave Myself Time" at 1601 NE Martin Luther King Jr. Boulevard. Created by local duo Rather Severe in collaboration with Fontana, it fights the stigma of depression.

A PLACE CALLED HOME

Map 6; 7000 NE Airport Way, Northeast Portland; ///axed.arena.finest

On arrival at Portland's airport, locals and new arrivals alike stop dead in their tracks. The reason? This super-colorful mural. Celebrating the city's marginalized communities, it depicts a variety of underappreciated characters in the city's history, including the Shoshone-Bannock storyteller Ed Edmo and pioneering blues guitarist Norman Sylvester.

Movie Theaters

If rain strikes (inevitable here), Portland's countless historic movie theaters come into their own. Come to catch a new indie film or the latest blockbuster – or simply to gawp at the old-school architecture.

LIVING ROOM THEATERS

Map 1; 341 SW 10th Avenue, Downtown; ///deck.issued.bound; https://pdx.livingroomtheaters.com

What's better than a movie? Dinner and a movie, that's what. Luckily, the Living Room combines both into one delightful package. It's no surprise, then, that it's a popular spot for date nights. Artsy couples come here on the regular to watch indie movies and foreign-language films, and to chow down on tasty grub with film-pun names (think Inglorious Bratwursts and Wild Wild Southwest Salad).

LAURELHURST THEATER

Map 3; 2735 E Burnside Street, Kerns; ///ages.glue.squad; www.laurelhursttheater.com

This 1920s movie theater is an icon of the Kerns neighborhood, thanks to its huge, Art Deco neon sign. Movie buffs are lured here nightly by its vivid glow and by the promise of super-cheap tickets. As well

Grab a beer to enjoy with your movie. The Laurelhurst has lots of local brews, including Breakside *(p71)*, on tap.

as mainstream movies, the theater screens more offbeat flicks, such as cheesy B movies (with film-goers encouraged to yell out one-liners) and cinematic classics.

THE BAGDAD THEATER & PUB

Map 5; 3702 SE Hawthorne Boulevard, Sunnyside;
///bench.exchanges.goad; www.mcmenamins.com/bagdad-theater-pub

Plucked from the grand age of cinema, this 1927 movie theater is a total beauty. There's a definite Middle Eastern vibe here, thanks to the Bagdad's barreled arches, eye-catching mosaics, and glowing lanterns. Join Sunnyside locals as they nestle down in the super-comfy rocker seats – choose one on the vaulted balcony for the best view – and get ready to watch the newest blockbuster.

>> **Don't leave without** grabbing a bite to eat in the attached pub before you head in; the pizza is pretty good.

CINEMA 21

Map 2; 616 NW 21st Avenue, Nob Hill; ///hears.love.cages;
www.cinema21.com

This historic cinema is at the beating heart of Portland's movie culture. It premieres important films (such as *Moonlight* and *Crouching Tiger, Hidden Dragon*); holds talks by renowned filmmakers; and hosts major events like the Portland Queer Film Festival. On any given evening, intellectuals, film students, and creatives flock here to catch the latest art-house and foreign-language films.

Solo, Pair, Crowd

Portland is bursting with awesome cinemas just perfect for movie nights, whoever you're hanging with.

FLYING SOLO
Weekday showings
During the week, the Regal cinema in Fox Tower is pretty quiet. Kickback here with mainstream films and indie flicks – you'll probably have the entire theater to yourself.

IN A PAIR
Get comfy
Showing all the newest releases, Studio One Theaters swaps out the usual cinema seats for super-comfy seats. Besties can grab squishy armchairs, while couples can get cozy on the loveseats.

FOR A CROWD
Room to maneuver
There are lots of reasons to love the Kennedy School Theater: fresh popcorn, a mixed program of new movies and much-loved classics, and cheap tickets. Plus, there's plenty of seats – making it a good bet for big gangs of friends.

HOLLYWOOD THEATRE

Map 4; 4122 NE Sandy Boulevard, Hollywood; ///crisp.sculpture.invent;
www.hollywoodtheatre.org

With its landmark flashing sign and striking, you-can't-miss-it
Spanish Colonial-inspired exterior, the Hollywood sure knows how
to attract attention. But this isn't a case of style over substance: the
almost 100-year-old cinema is famed for first-run screenings of
smaller indie films, and hosts film festivals with themes like kung
fu and queer horror. It also provides regular support for aspiring
local filmmakers. No wonder it's such a beloved part of the
Hollywood neighborhood.

» Don't leave without booking in for B-Movie Bingo (first Tuesday of
the month), where you'll tick-off B-movie clichés from your bingo card
as you watch low-budget gems.

THE ACADEMY THEATER

Map 5; 7818 SE Stark Street, Montavilla; ///author.edgy.flats;
https://academytheaterpdx.com

The Academy might be the baby of Portland's clutch of indie
theaters, having first opened its doors in the mid-20th century, but
that doesn't mean it can't hold its own against its more vintage
siblings. Film buffs adore this little theater for its snug, red-curtained
rooms, where they can catch the newest blockbusters while sipping
on craft beer and eating pizza slices (served piping hot from nearby
Flying Pie Pizzeria). The best thing about the Academy, though,
is its screenings of classic movies and all-time favorites, with
everything from *Psycho* to *Clueless* lighting up the big screen.

Indie Galleries

Portlanders love to push the boundaries and express themselves through art. Here, contemporary pieces – often with a social or political angle – are displayed in uber-cool spaces.

FULLER ROSEN GALLERY

Map 2; 1928 NW Lovejoy Street, Nob Hill; ///guises.racing.list; www.fullerrosen.com

This queer-owned gallery is all about tackling urgent, modern-day issues. The exhibitions – created by emerging artists – focus on diverse topics, such as environmental upheaval and the representations of trans people in pop culture. Expect a diverse crowd, too: arty retirees, tattooed 20-somethings, and creative families all fill the space.

MELANIE FLOOD PROJECTS

Map 1; 420 SW Washington Street, Downtown; ///march.milk.snack; www.melaniefloodprojects.com

Back in 2008, art lover and photographer Melanie Flood set up an artists' space in her Brooklyn apartment in New York City. Fast-forward a couple of years (and a move to the other side of the country) and this tiny, bright gallery – known as MFP to locals –

was born. Its welcoming vibe, works by up-and-coming artists, and varied lineup (exhibitions change monthly) mean that this is a spot art lovers end up visiting again and again.

CARNATION CONTEMPORARY

Map 6; 8371 N Interstate Avenue, Kenton; ///transmitted.shell.across;
www.carnationcontemporary.com

Provocative, thought-inducing pieces are the name of the game at Carnation Contemporary, an ultramodern gallery set up by a collective of Portland artists. Here, a vibrant young crowd wander across the polished concrete floor, pausing to discuss the highly conceptual contemporary pieces, which range from 3-D printed sculptures to abstract paintings.

» **Don't leave without** browsing the gallery's store, which has various original works for sale by Carnation artists.

Morrison Street Minigallery (3229 SE Morrison Street) is easy to miss. Set up by Alissa and Jerry Tran just outside of their Victorian-style home in Sunnyside, this diminutive gallery is housed in a foot-long white box. Yes, the space is small (okay, *really* small), but that doesn't stop local artists or the couple themselves filling it with quirky pieces. Past exhibits have included crocheted cacti, ceramic cephalopods, and paintings of iconic women, such as Ruth Bader Ginsberg.

RADIUS ART STUDIO

Map 3; 2324 SE Belmont Street, Buckman; ///lands.ocean.mild;
www.radiusstudio.org

Owned by working artist Korin Schneider, Radius Art Studio is a community space for ceramic artists. Its gallery-shop is filled with cute ornaments, mugs, and more, all handmade by local potters. Fancy getting your hands dirty? The studio offers pottery classes, too.

OREGON CENTER FOR CONTEMPORARY ART

Map 6; 8371 N Interstate Avenue, Kenton;
///lasts.player.olive; www.oregoncontemporary.org

This nonprofit gallery draws the creative crowds to North Portland with its lofty gallery space and contemporary exhibits, which often highlight marginalized voices. Oh, and it also hosts the Portland Biennial, a major celebration of Oregon artists. What's not to love?

NATIONALE

Map 3; 15 SE 22nd Avenue, Buckman; ///thing.adults.hype;
www.nationale.us

Come the weekend, Buckman locals and beyond can be found at this cool little gallery. They come to gaze at the colorful, culture-focused works, which often deal with important issues, such as the erasure of Black figures throughout history.

» Don't leave without visiting the attached shop, which stocks a carefully curated selection of books, vinyl, and locally made items.

Liked by the locals

"Galleries in Portland crop up anywhere – a back-alley warehouse, a filmmaker's home, a chicken coop. Eclectic islands of scenes and communities, each is guided by the personal focus of its respective curators or collectives."

SUZETTE SMITH, ARTS AND CULTURE EDITOR
AT THE PORTLAND MERCURY

Quirky Collections

The city doesn't have the motto "Keep Portland Weird" for nothing. There are countless kooky collections here, from museums dedicated to vacuums (yep, you read that right) to gatherings of fantastical objects.

PORTLAND PUPPET MUSEUM

Map 6; 906 SE Umatilla Street, Sellwood-Moreland; ///hours.spray.rash;
www.puppetmuseum.com

Puppets – folks either love 'em or hate 'em. If you're in the latter camp, then definitely steer clear of this offbeat museum, every inch of which is crammed with marionettes, dummies, and more. It's the personal collection of the welcoming Steven Overton, a master puppeteer who's been designing, making, and collecting puppets for over 50 years. He puts on shows, too, so you can see the puppets in action.

ZYMOGLYPHIC MUSEUM

Map 5; 6225 SE Alder Street, Mount Tabor;
///kinks.dozen.liked; www.zymoglyphic.org

If any one place sums up the city's love of the wacky and the weird, it's the Zymoglyphic Museum. This surreal cabinet of curiosities has the vibe of an eccentric Victorian collector's study. Fantastical objects are dotted on every surface: think bird skeletons in rickety wire carts and "tree gnomes" made with bark and shells. These dreamlike items are the work of the museum's imaginative proprietor, Jim Stewart, who crafts them himself from largely natural materials. Still not sure what it's all about? We don't blame you, but all the more reason to visit this quirky collection (open Sundays) for yourself.

BILLY GALAXY

Map 1; 912 W Burnside Street, Downtown;
///that.outfit.cherry; www.billygalaxy.com

Sure, it's technically a shop, but this collection of vintage toys is so expertly curated that it feels like a museum. Hardcore collectors can be found raking the shelves for rare finds, while curious out-of-towners (who often wander in by mistake) get a serious nostalgia hit from the Star Wars action figures and old-school Barbie dolls.

» Don't leave without picking up a collectible to take home, whether that's an old movie poster or a Smurf Christmas tree decoration.

STARK'S VACUUM MUSEUM

Map 3; 107 NE Grand Avenue, Buckman; ///goat.happen.beans;
www.starks.com/about/vacuum-museum

Hidden within Stark's Vacuums store, this unusual museum celebrates the humble vacuum cleaner. Chat to well-versed staff about this household tool's storied history, then take a peek at the colorful display of vacuums through the ages. You'll leave with a newfound respect for your vacuum (and probably some new bags for it, too).

NATIONAL HAT MUSEUM

Map 3; 1928 SE Ladd Avenue, Ladd's Addition; ///ozone.others.open;
www.thehatmuseum.com

Hats, hats, and – wait for it – more hats. That's what you'll find at this kooky museum, home to almost 2,200 different head toppers. Accessory-obsessed Portlanders come here to drool over the vast collection, with everything from vintage Edwardian to retro 1960s styles on display. There's even a Thanksgiving table hat that sings.

FREAKYBUTTRUE PECULIARIUM

Map 2; 2234 NW Thurman Street, Slabtown;
///apples.upper.fall; www.peculiarium.com

This place almost defies description – but normal it ain't. Born from the owners' love of urban legends, cryptids, and the mysterious, this "anti-museum" is filled with some truly bizarre bits and bobs. Looking for a

Shh!

On McNamee Road, just outside of Portland, there's an old trestle railway bridge. And under this bridge, as you might expect, lives a colony of trolls. But these aren't the fearsome creatures of Scandi legend. Instead you'll find countless cute Troll Dolls, with huge smiles and colorful tufted hair. No one is quite sure how the tradition started, but local residents have been adding these cheerful toys to the wooden slatted supports beneath the bridge for nearly two decades.

massive Bigfoot statue? It's here. A bathtub full of plastic guts? You got it. Plus, some exhibits are interactive, so if you've ever wondered what it's like to be buried alive, no problem – there's a simulator for that.

MOVIE MADNESS VIDEO

Map 5; 4320 SE Belmont Street, Sunnyside;
///whips.second.deep; www.moviemadness.org

When Movie Madness was threatened with closure in 2017, the community (plus the nonprofit Hollywood Theatre *(p127)*) rallied to save it. And no wonder they did – this old-school video store is a Portland institution. With over 80,000 movies on DVD, Blu-ray, and even super-retro VHS, it's a veritable archive of cinema. Movie buffs come here to wander the endless rows of films and to nerd out over the displays of eclectic movie memorabilia: check out Basil Rathbone's doublet from the 1936 *Romeo and Juliet* and the knife from *Psycho*.

OMSI AFTER DARK

Map 3; 1945 SE Water Avenue, Hosford-Abernethy;
///acted.trail.stews; www.omsi.edu

While schoolkids might reign supreme during the day, the Oregon Museum of Science and Industry is for adults only when dusk falls. The monthly OMSI After Dark events are pretty cool: DJs spin beats while curious over-21s, drinks in hand, learn about robots or shoot off water rockets – all without lines of kids forming behind them.

» Don't leave without booking in for one of the museum's foodie-focused maker workshops to learn all about things like cheese making.

An arty afternoon in the
Alberta Arts District

Alberta has had a troubled past. From the mid-20th century, the march of gentrification led to tension in this historically Black neighborhood, with crime, neglect, and racism becoming big issues. From the 1990s, community groups made efforts to revitalize the area, decorating the main drag with murals and introducing monthly Art Walks. Now Alberta is awash with public art, including pieces that show the history of the neighborhood's Black community.

WOODLAWN

NORTHEAST 13TH AVENUE

Dotted throughout the area are **Black Heritage Markers**, *public art markers that tell the story of Alberta's Black community.*

5

End the afternoon at the ALBERTA STREET PUB
Feeling hungry? Pull up a seat in this old-school watering hole and devour one of its hearty, comfort food dishes, washed down with a pint, of course. There's often local live music here, too.

NORTHEAST 13TH AVENUE

NORTHEAST

1. Black United Fund Building
2828 NE Alberta Street, Alberta; www.bufor.org
///stacks.cling.sport

2. Antler Gallery
2728 NE Alberta Street, Alberta; www.antlerpdx.com
///comical.gifted.minus

3. Just Bob
2403 NE Alberta Street, Alberta; www.justbob pdx.com
///runner.thigh.nasal

4. Six Strong
1500 NE Alberta Street, Alberta; www.tovcoffee.com
///tower.damp.tower

5. Alberta Street Pub
1036 NE Alberta Street, Alberta; www.alberta streetpub.com
///thanks.mobile.bets

📍 **Last Thursday**
///leap.meant.swaps

📍 **Black Heritage Markers**
///mops.jars.closes

NORTHEAST AVENUE
AVENUE
AVENUE
NORTHEAST AINSWORTH STREET

22ND
27TH
31ST
CONCORDIA

Alberta Park

NORTHEAST
NORTHEAST
NORTHEAST

NORTHEAST KILLINGSWORTH STREET

**…ause by the mural
…X STRONG**

…ound in the Alberta
…o-op parking lot,
…ese six diverse
…anels depict stories of
…male empowerment.

*Last Thursday is an
energetic monthly street
fair that sees Northeast
Alberta Street come
alive with art and
music performances.*

**Pop into the
ANTLER GALLERY**

Check out the beautiful
nature-inspired pieces
for sale here; the works
have been curated from
around the world.

4 — NORTHEAST ALBERTA STREET — 3 — 2 — 1

ALBERTA

**Make a pit stop at
JUST BOB**

Grab a coffee and admire the
art-lined walls here, then pop
outside to see the painting of a
stag and wolf splashed across
The Alleyway Bar next door.

**Admire the mural on the
BLACK UNITED
FUND BUILDING**

This colorful artwork
honors historically significant
Black women, such as
author Coretta Scott King.
Around the corner, six murals
celebrate the area's history,
including one depicting some
of its Indigenous peoples,
the Chinook and Kalapuya.

AVENUE
27TH
NORTHEAST

NORTHEAST PRESCOTT STREET

AVENUE

NORTHEAST

24TH

NORTHEAST MASON STREET

NORTHEAST

…GEWOOD DRIVE

ALAMEDA

0 meters 400
0 yards 400

NIGHTLIFE

Portland likes to get a little weird (or is that weirder?) once the sun sets. From burlesque book readings to subversive improv acts, the city's nightlife is all about self-expression.

Games Night

Portland loves to play. Locals enjoy nothing better than a hardcore Dungeons & Dragons sesh, an energetic sing-off, or a night spent playing vintage video games – all with a drink in hand, of course.

GROUND KONTROL

Map 1; 115 NW 5th Avenue, Old Town/Chinatown;
///duck.became.spring; www.groundkontrol.com

At Portland's original "barcade," sentimental locals relive the good ol' days on the neon-lit, quarter-fueled games – think Street Fighter II, Ms. Pac Man, and Teenage Mutant Ninja Turtles. If that's not enough wallet-draining nostalgia, try one of the retro cocktails: it's pretty fun to sip on a Mario Kart-inspired Banana Spin Out while attempting to kill aliens on Space Invaders.

BABY KETTEN KLUB

Map 5; 2433 SE Powell Boulevard, Hosford-Abernethy;
///oath.wedge.good; www.babyketten.com

Baby Ketten has everything you'd ever want from a karaoke bar: a massive song list, superb sound quality, and, most importantly, cheap drinks. Add to this laser lights and a smoke machine, and

Singing is hungry work. Happily, the bar's vegan food, including the jumbo chilidawg, is totally delicious. your inner diva will have you up singing "I Will Survive" before you know it. More of an introvert? Hide yourself away in one of the 70s- or 80s-style private rooms.

QUARTERWORLD

Map 5; 4811 SE Hawthorne Boulevard, Mount Tabor;
///bumps.groups.less; www.quarterworldarcade.com

An homage to the 90s era, QuarterWorld is all about the variety. At this glowing arcade, gaggles of girlfriends kick ass on Street Fighter II Turbo, beanie-wearing hipsters try to level up on Donkey Kong, and pinballers play away to the chimes, whirls, and blasts of the bar's Iron Man- or Dr. Who-themed machines. Not sure where to start? Try Ninja Baseball Bat Man, a super-rare offering, or test out the biceps on Boxer's punch bag.

» Don't leave without seeing a show by the arcade's musical Tesla coil. Nicknamed "Tessi," its lightning bolts produce music, which appropriately sounds like the 8-bit soundtracks from classic video games.

RIALTO

Map 1; 529 SW 4th Avenue, Downtown; ///class.mugs.habit;
www.rialto-poolroom.com

This down-to-earth spot sees an eclectic mix of tipsy office workers and eager Portland State students shooting billiards on the grassy green tables. Grab a drink at the well-stocked bar and, taking your cue (pun intended), join in the fun.

Solo, Pair, Crowd

Portland has plenty of places where you and your friends can embrace your inner kids on a nostalgic night out.

FLYING SOLO

Challenge accepted

The tiny Retro Game Bar serves up all your favorite video games from the 70s, 80s, and 90s. Play on one of the consoles at the bar, or challenge a fellow player to a game of Mario Kart or Super Smash Bros.

IN A PAIR

Ping-pong with a pal

Found in a light and bright space, Pips & Bounce is Portland's beloved ping-pong social club. With craft cocktails, an outdoor patio, and five tables, it's the perfect place for a night out with the bestie.

FOR A CROWD

Games galore

Punch Bowl Social takes up the entire 3rd floor of Pioneer Place Mall. There's video games, bowling, karaoke, and more, making it the perfect weekend hangout for you and your posse.

MOX BOARDING HOUSE

Map 2; 1938 W Burnside Street, Goose Hollow; ///remark.vine.sector; www.moxboardinghouse.com

Board games are for life, not just for Christmas – and Mox can prove it. The wooden tables at this Parisian-inspired gaming hall are filled nightly with all sorts of Portlanders, lured here by the vast selection of games and craft beer-stocked bar. Here, first-timers play old school faves (hello Monopoly and Risk), while the hardcore gamers battle it out over role-playing offerings such as Dungeons & Dragons and Magic: The Gathering. Grab a drink and join in the fun – there's nothing like an evening spent fighting monsters and casting spells, right?

>> Don't leave without picking up a new addition to your board game cupboard at home. Mox has an attached retail store that's piled high with every table-top game you could dream of.

WEDGEHEAD

Map 4; 3728 NE Sandy Boulevard, Hollywood; ///junior.suffer.fuzzy; www.wedgeheadpdx.com

Once a rowdy punk club, Wedgehead is now a magnet for lovers of pinball, who flock here to hone their skills. Inside, the dark space is lit by the glow of themed machines, including options dedicated to Tron, Star Trek, and (in a nod to the bar's punk past) the Ramones. While the whiz, ping, and clatter of balls (not to mention the thumping music) ring out around you, grab a cheap tallboy and pit your wits and your wrists against Wedgehead's fearsome Godzilla or vintage Bally machines.

Culture Live

This city sure knows how to shake things up on stage. From provocative theater productions to subversive comedy shows, there's always something unique on the cards.

HELIUM CLUB

Map 3; 1510 SE 9th Avenue, Hosford-Abernethy; ///stress.guides.patio; https://portland.heliumcomedy.com

Helium might be Portland's premier comedy club, but it isn't big or showy – and that's what makes it great. With café-style seating around a small wooden stage, this intimate spot gets you up close with the comedians, whether it's newbies at their first open mic night or big-name comics tearing up the stage. Just remember to avoid the front row (unless you're keen for a bit of audience participation, that is).

FUNHOUSE LOUNGE

Map 3; 2432 SE 11th Avenue, Hosford-Abernethy; ///notion.urgent.units; www.funhouselounge.com

The Funhouse Lounge looks like a traditional theater, but its shows are far from conventional. Past performances have included an unscripted musical version of *Star Trek: The Next Generation*, improv nights run by Mistress, the lounge's very own dominatrix, and jazz-themed comedy shows. Look out for the hilarious rehashes of classic films, too, like *Die Hard* or *Pulp Fiction*.

» **Don't leave without** visiting the unique (read: terrifying) Clown Room, decked out with a colorful array of clown portraits.

THE SIREN THEATER
Map 1; 315 NW Davis Street, Old Town/Chinatown;
///dangerously.deny.lasted; www.sirentheater.com

In 2015, kick-ass comedian Shelley McLendon set up this snug theater as a permanent home for her imaginative performance studio, Bad Reputation Productions. Since then it's gone from strength to strength – no surprise, given its epic lineup of out-of-the-ordinary sketch comedy, stand-up, and performance acts. Expect transgressive shows, with issues of racism, sexism, and homophobia addressed through the lens of comedy. A highlight? Minority Retort: this local stand-up showcase, exclusively featuring comedians of color, serves up witty dollops of laugh-out-loud comedy.

Try it!
BECOME A COMEDIAN

The Siren Theater offers comedy classes, covering things like musical improv and sketch comedy. There's even an intensive yearly course run by Shelley herself. Check out the website for a full list.

Liked by the locals

"PCS is a pulsating center of live art. Over and over it gives Portlanders a chance to discover themselves in new and meaningful ways, whether by cracking up, gasping with their seat mate, or sobbing out loud."

LAUREN MODICA, OREGON SHAKESPEARE FESTIVAL AND PORTLAND ACTOR

ALBERTA ROSE THEATRE

Map 4; 3000 NE Alberta Street, Concordia;
///shirts.events.loved; www.albertarosetheatre.com

This treasured vintage theater survived the pandemic thanks to its loyal fans, who donated and streamed concerts online. It's easy to see why it's so loved: the Alberta Rose is overflowing with variety, from performances by indie songwriters to poetry readings.

PORTLAND CENTER STAGE

Map 1; 128 NW 11th Avenue, Pearl District;
///actor.normal.puts; www.pcs.org

The big hitter of the city's theater scene, Portland Center Stage (PCS) has it all: Broadway shows, genre-bending plays, and avant-garde drag performances. Out-of-towners come here for big hits like *Rent* and *Oklahoma!*, while regulars rock up for the theater's experimental plays, often produced by local writers and creators.

» Don't leave without grabbing a glass of locally made bubbly or beer at the stylish Armory Bar.

ARTISTS REPERTORY THEATER

Map 1; 128 NW 11th Avenue, Pearl District;
///actor.normal.puts; www.artistsrep.org

Sharing a space with PCS, this theater company offers provocative performances, often with powerful social and political commentary. Catch a modern retelling of *Richard III* set in high school, or a satire of American capitalism via the experience of fast-food production.

LGBTQ+ Scene

Thanks to its long history of gay rights activism, Portland today has a super-welcoming LGBTQ+ scene. There's something for everyone here, from uber-inclusive strip clubs to laid-back bars.

CRUSH BAR

Map 3; 1400 SE Morrison Street, Buckman;
///closes.photos.sits; www.crushbar.com

Low-key, laid-back, and welcoming: that's Crush. At this LGBTQ+ bar and café, friendly staff serve up kick-ass cocktails, big smiles, and even bigger plates of warming comfort food (the nachos are to die for). Grab a ginger-tastic Crush Mule and catch a mesmerizing drag or burlesque show, or get chatting with the folks at the table next to you. You'll feel so at home, it might be difficult to leave.

CC SLAUGHTERS

Map 1; 219 NW Davis Street, Old Town/Chinatown;
///sentences.lock.flock; www.ccslaughterspdx.com

Possibly Portland's best nightclub, this much-loved spot has served the city's queer community for four fabulous decades. Each night, a cool crowd sips martinis in the Rainbow Room before busting some

Once you've watched the drag queens strut their stuff, remember to offer them a tip – it's the done thing.

moves on the dance floor. Come here for Thursty Thursdays, a night dedicated to the city's trans community, or pop by on Fridays for the bar's legendary drag show.

STAG PDX

Map 1; 317 NW Broadway, Pearl District;
///pushes.mostly.blog; www.stagportland.com

This super-inclusive gay strip club celebrates all sexual orientations and gender expressions. Ripped men regularly bare it all here, but Stag also hosts lesbian nights and body positivity nights. It's also one of the only clubs in the US to host trans strip nights. Catch one of the shows and then boogie the night away to DJ sets spun by drag queens.

SCANDALS

Map 1; 1125 SW Harvey Milk Street, Downtown;
///dimes.print.cape; www.scandalspdx.com

Self-dubbed Portland's "Gay Cheers," Scandals has collected a troop of loyal locals over the past 40-plus years. And no wonder: this relaxed bar is all about cheap drinks, chilled vibes, and a community feel. Join the regulars as they laze on the large outdoor patio or sing their hearts out come karaoke night (that's on Tuesdays, FYI). One thing's for sure: by the end of the night, you'll know everyone's names.
» Don't leave without booking in for "Brunch with the Boys" on the weekend – all dishes are priced at $5 and under.

Liked by the locals

"When we started in 1967, drag wasn't anywhere in Portland. But now drag queens are everywhere – you can't throw a cat down the street without hitting a drag queen. And that's great, because that's what we worked for, to make it work and make it accepted."

DARCELLE, OWNER OF DARCELLE XV SHOWPLACE

DARCELLE XV SHOWPLACE

Map 1; 208 NW 3rd Avenue, Old Town/Chinatown;
///scam.brush.putty; www.darcellexv.com

Darcelle's is a Portland institution. Set up by the vivacious Darcelle herself (at 91, the world's oldest drag queen), this snug theater hosts the West Coast's longest-running drag show. Expect Whitney Houston lip-syncing, renditions of the Time Warp, and a whole lot of glitzy fun.

» Don't leave without booking in for the Sunday Funday Drag Queen Brunch, hosted by megastar drag queen Poison Waters.

EAGLE

Map 6; 835 N Lombard Street, Piedmont;
///pillow.wage.pint; www.eagleportland.com

Portland's bear and leather bar loves to play dress-up. This spot's famous themed nights see punters rock up in everything from leather chaps to construction worker costumes to jock straps only (often for free entry). The bar also offers BBQs, karaoke nights, and (X-rated) movie screenings.

THE QUEEN'S HEAD

Map 1; 19 SW 2nd Avenue, Downtown; ///honest.pine.spirit;
www.thequeensheadpdx.com

A newer kid on the block, this queer bar is all about live shows: think musical drag acts and queer talent comps, with a few burlesque performances thrown in. The only way to make your night better is to grab one of the bar's signature cocktails — we'll have a Calamity Jane.

Live Music

The home of quirky indie acts and acclaimed artists alike (including the Dandy Warhols and Eliot Smith), Portland is a magnet for great music, with local musicians and cool venues at the heart of the scene.

WONDER BALLROOM

Map 4; 128 NE Russell Street, Eliot; ///quiet.hero.risk; www.wonderballroom.com

Almost 800 gig-goers can fit inside this Mission Revival building, but it never seems that way – in fact, concerts at the Wonder Ballroom feel utterly intimate. All the better for fans of the famous, who come here to get up close to the big-name acts gracing the stag (think Lizzo and Lady Gaga). Superstars aside, the venue also hosts performances by alternative blues bands, local folk musicians, and more.

MISSISSIPPI STUDIOS

Map 4; 3939 N Mississippi Avenue, Boise; ///urgent.kicked.gains; www.mississippistudios.com

Follow in-the-know music lovers to this converted Baptist church (known for its impeccable sound quality) and you may just find your new favorite band. While music heavyweights do perform here, owners Jim Brunberg and Ben Landsverk, themselves musicians and recording artists, take pride in crafting a lineup that really celebrates local, indie artists. Grab a beer, get cozy with the locals (it can get pretty rammed), and discover Portland's next big thing.

DOUG FIR LOUNGE

Map 3; 830 E Burnside Street, Buckman;
///thigh.lived.estate; www.dougfirlounge.com

The walls of this subterranean space are lined by huge cabin-style tree logs – hence the name, and the great acoustics. There's a genre-spanning spectrum of music on offer here (although Doug Fir's biggest love is definitely rock). On any given night, an eclectic mix of locals can be found swaying to folk melodies, bouncing around to dance-punk, or nodding energetically to the beats of indie rock.

» Don't leave without admiring the quirky design of the upstairs bar, which looks like a cross between a space ship and a rustic cabin.

EDGEFIELD

Map 6; 2126 SW Halsey Street, Troutdale; ///plot.years.snake;
www.mcmenamins.com/edgefield

Come summer, Portlanders head to Edgefield. As well as a hotel and vineyard, this vast farm-turned-resort is home to an epic outdoor stage that's hosted acts like Willie Nelson and Portugal. The Man. Head here on a balmy summer evening with a group of good friends, spread a blanket out on the grass, and watch as your favorite musicians rock out as the sun sets.

Solo, Pair, Crowd

No matter if it's just you and the music, or you and your friends, there's a venue ready and waiting.

FLYING SOLO
Cozy up
Small and casual, the showroom at Kelly's Olympian (located in a side room off the main bar) hosts regular live music. Perfect for when you fancy taking yourself on a date.

IN A PAIR
Expand your horizons
Once a movie house and a burlesque theater, the Star Theater today is a rocking 500-seat music venue. You and your best bud are guaranteed to find a new favorite rock, jazz, or electronic band here.

FOR A CROWD
Bounce across the ballroom
Portland's famous Crystal Ballroom *(p116)* has a "floating" dance floor perfect for bouncy boogying and multiple bars for mid-gig drinks. Head here with a whole group of mates to catch everything from rap to indie pop.

REVOLUTION HALL

Map 3; 1300 SE Stark Street, Buckman;
///counts.hired.dress; www.revolutionhall.com

This quirky venue is all about old-school charm – literally, since it's housed inside an old high school. Walking into the auditorium, with its rows of original wooden seats, you half expect a weary principal to appear on stage. Instead, a buzzing mix of folk, indie rock, and pop acts will have you dancing till dawn. Who said school wasn't cool?

» Don't leave without catching a 360-degree view of the Portland skyline from the hall's Roof Deck Terrace.

ALADDIN

Map 3; 2017 SE Milwaukie Avenue, Hosford-Abernethy;
///link.oils.diary; www.aladdin-theater.com

Vaudeville hall, film house, X-rated movie theater: the Aladdin has been a lot of things. These days the charming 1920s venue is all about staging thoroughly modern concerts. Rock, jazz, pop, rap – you name it, it's on the lineup.

ARLENE SCHNITZER CONCERT HALL

Map 1; 1037 SW Broadway, Downtown; ///give.cares.views;
www.portland5.com/arlene-schnitzer-concert-hall

When Portlanders' parents come to visit, they treat them to a classical concert at this elegant spot. Home of the Oregon Symphony, the Schnitz, as locals call it, is guaranteed to impress the rents with its state-of-the-art acoustics and opulent interior, including crystal chandeliers.

Late-Night Entertainment

Portland gets its freak on after dark. Whether you're watching budget wrestling, catching a tantalizing burlesque show, or singing karaoke backed up by strippers, no two nights in Portland are the same.

CLINTON STREET THEATER

Map 3; 2522 SE Clinton Street, Richmond;
///leads.cove.silks; www.cstpdx.com

Every Saturday at midnight, this indie theater transforms into a den of outrageousness thanks to *The Rocky Horror Picture Show*. Played here weekly since 1978, this cult classic is hosted by the Clinton Street Cabaret, who give a raunchy performance as the movie plays behind them. You'll need your gold hotpants – dressing up is de rigueur.

BLUE COLLAR WRESTLING

Map 6; 7525 N Richmond Avenue, St Johns; ///derogatory.howler.smooth

Ever seen a lycra-clad mom lay a dropkick? Or watched a grease-stained mechanic serve up a powerbomb? Well you can at Blue Collar Wrestling (BCW to its regulars). At one of these shows, avid wrestling fans pile into The Colony (an old Mid-Century ballroom) to cheer as folk with names like Meat and Badd Blood grapple with each other – all while dressed in DIY costumes.

DEVILS POINT

Map 5; 5305 SE Foster Road, Foster-Powell;
///fumes.peanut.draw; www.devilspointbar.com

Yep, this is a strip club. But how could we miss it? After all, Portland has more stripper joints per capita than any other US city, and Devils Point is one of its best. This rock 'n' roll spot attracts punks, goths, and rockers of all stripes, as well as a steady stream of stupefied tourists. And why do they come? For Stripperoke, of course. Every Sunday a warbling rockstar wannabe bleats out their favorite song between two heavy chains, while a stripper or two dances behind them on stage. Rock on.

» Don't leave without tipping the talented dancers; the rule is at least $1 per dancer, per song.

Cycle through the night on the Midnight Mystery Ride *(www. midnightmysteryride.wordpress. com)*. On the second Monday of each month, this offbeat bicycle tour meets at a pre-arranged spot at midnight, before following an unspoken route to a mysterious location. Spoiler alert: it's usually a bar.

MARY'S CLUB

Map 1; 503 W Burnside Street, Old Town/Chinatown;
///wider.expect.view; www.marysclub.com

Okay, yes, this is another strip club (in fact, it's technically the oldest one in the city). But aside from the obvious touchstones (like the stripper poles), this family-run, women-owned spot feels more like a trendy bar than your "typical" strip club. For one thing, the decor is less dingy, more stylish (think high-ceilings and subway-tiled walls). For another, it's filled with an eclectic mix of folk (pretty much 50:50 men and women) who sip on their drinks as they watch tattooed women dance to their own beat – literally, as the dancers choose the songs.

BOOKLOVER'S BURLESQUE

Map 4; 3000 NE Alberta Street, Alberta Arts District;
///doll.hatch.same; www.bookloversburlesque.com

"Sexy" and "thrilling" aren't words that spring to mind when you think of book readings, right? But that's because you've never been to Booklover's Burlesque. At this tantalizing literary salon, readings

Try it!
BE MORE BURLESQUE

ShowGirl Temple's FriYay Burlesque is a sassy introduction to this sensual art form (www.showgirltemple.com). These body-positive classes will have you shimmying, shaking, and strutting in no time.

of poetry, fiction, memoir, and beyond (basically, any genre goes) are followed by sensual and creative burlesque, boylesque, and draglesque performances inspired by the piece. You might hear "Venus In Furs" dictated by a buxom drag queen, or an extract from a Gothic novel read aloud by a lingerie-clad performer. Whatever is on the cards, you'll leave feeling empowered and titillated – and with a newfound perspective on some of your favorite works.

» **Don't leave without** checking the salon's website to find out about upcoming performances and their locations. While most events are held at the Alberta Rose Theatre, other venues are also used.

SINFERNO CABARET @ DANTE'S

Map 1; 350 W Burnside Street, Old Town/Chinatown;
///heats.fakes.towers; www.danteslive.com

Dante's is an earnest, hell-themed bar at the edge of Old Town with lived-in charm and scumbag-punk cred galore. Most nights you'll find aging scenesters chain-smoking out front while rebooted alt-rockers and up-and-coming metal bands push the sound system to its limits. But that's not the best thing about Dante's – that goes to Sinferno Cabaret, held here every Sunday. Each debauched show is a unique mash-up of burlesque dancers, fire spinners, DJ sets, and more. One night, one of the bartenders might be seen juggling knives in bondage gear. Another evening, everyone's favorite Suicide Girl could ride by on a unicycle, wearing nothing but a thong and a few pieces of electrical tape. If you're fixing to do as the city's motto dictates and "Keep Portland Weird," this is certainly a great place to start.

NORTHWEST

EVERETT STREET

NORTHWEST 5TH AVENUE

Get the party started at
DARCELLE XV SHOWPLACE
Catch a fun-filled drag show at this iconic spot, hosted by 91-year-old Darcelle – the world's oldest drag queen.

3

NORTHWEST DAVIS STREET

NORTHWEST 4TH AVENUE

CHINATOWN

NORTHWEST 3RD AVENUE

Get your game on at
GROUND KONTROL
Play neon-lit, vintage arcade games, while sipping retro cocktails at Portland's orginal barcade.

2

NORTHWEST

COUCH STREET

Start your night at
TOPE
Chow down on tasty tacos and sip on tequila and mezcal drinks at this cool spot. The sweeping views from the patio balcony aren't bad either.

1

0 meters	50
0 yards	50

WEST BURNSIDE STREET

*Su Chinese
Garden*

An entertaining evening in
Old Town/
Chinatown

The birthplace of Portland in the mid-19th century, this area became a bustling Chinatown around the 1870s. Home to gambling dens, brothels, and opium dens, it was a place where shaking the norms of society was seen as acceptable – even applauded. Fast-forward almost 200 years, and the neighborhood still has a reputation for hedonism, with a clutch of bars, clubs, and late-night venues dotting its streets.

**Dance till you drop in
CC SLAUGHTERS**
If you have the energy, head to this beloved LGBTQ+ nightclub to hit the dance floor and boogie the night away.

 4

Old Town Brewing is built above the **Shanghai Tunnels** *(p117), a series of passages that run beneath Chinatown.*

1. Tope
15 NW 4th Avenue,
Old Town/Chinatown;
www.thehoxton.com/
portland/tope-restaurant
///potato.crowd.fame

2. Ground Kontrol
115 NW 5th Avenue, Old Town/Chinatown; www.
groundkontrol.com
///duck.became.spring

3. Darcelle XV Showplace
208 NW 3rd Avenue,
Old Town/Chinatown;
www.darcellexv.com
///scam.brush.putty

4. CC Slaughters
219 NW Davis Street,
Old Town/Chinatown;
www.ccslaughterspdx.com
///sentences.lock.flock

NORTHWEST 2ND AVENUE

WEST   BURNSIDE   STREET

Shanghai Tunnels ///spit.hogs.couches

OUTDOORS

Portlanders love exploring the great outdoors – and no wonder. After all, the city is filled with pretty parks and has the stunning Pacific Northwest right on its doorstep.

Green Spaces

*Portland is one of America's greenest cities. From
the well-kept to the wild, the city's parks and gardens
are a big part of local life: the setting for picnics on
sunny days and drizzly walks when it rains.*

LAURELHURST PARK

**Map 5; enter at SE Cesar E Chavez Boulevard and Stark Street,
Laurelhurst; ///jump.silver.entertainer; www.portland.gov/parks**

There are two sides to this slice of green: the sporty and the chilled.
While Lillard fans shoot hoops on the basketball court and retirees
play games of tennis, those looking for a bit of peace stroll along
the quiet tree-lined paths. The park is busiest in summer, when the
lawns around the duck-filled pond are covered with picnicking
20-somethings – come early to grab a spot for you and your pals.

PORTLAND JAPANESE GARDEN

**Map 2; 611 SW Kingston Avenue, West Hills; ///pays.anyway.parent;
www.japanesegarden.org**

This garden was created as a gesture of friendship between the US
and Japan following World War II, so it's fitting that it's one of the most
peaceful spots in Portland. Worn-out 9-to-5-ers come to recharge

by its pretty koi ponds and zen gardens or to meditate to the melody of its tumbling waterfalls. Take a stroll beneath the garden's elegant Japanese maples – which shine verdant green in summer and glow brilliant orange in fall – for a break from the city.

» **Don't leave without** enjoying a pot of soothing matcha tea and views of the surrounding forest at the glass-walled Umami Café.

FOREST PARK

Map 6; enter at Forest Park NW PDX entrance at the end of NW Thurman Street, Forest Park; ///keeps.pets.link; www.forestparkconservancy.org/forest-park

As the sun rises, adventurous Portlanders looking to escape the hum of the city hurry toward this vast park (it's one of the largest urban forests in the US). Mountain bikers power up its gravel tracks, joggers scamper through the trees, and hikers clamber up its leg-burning hills. But don't think this park is just for outdoorsy types. Its leafy paths are also great for casual Sunday strolls, with plenty of wildlife to spy – if you're lucky, you might see a bald eagle, America's national symbol.

Try it!
CARE FOR THE FOREST

The Forest Park Conservancy runs a volunteer scheme to help keep the park in great shape. Don your eco-warrior suit (i.e. old clothes) and restore trails, remove invasive plants, and clear up litter.

TOM MCCALL WATERFRONT PARK

Map 1; enter at NW Couch Street and Pacific Highway W, Downtown;
///sticks.watch.frog; www.portland.gov/parks

Whatever the time of year, the paths of this pretty waterside park are liberally dotted with joggers, cyclists, and skaters, who zoom past laid-back locals taking in panoramic views of the Willamette River or snapping pics by the fountain. The best time to visit, though, is during spring, when the park's cherry trees burst into glorious bloom.

INTERNATIONAL ROSE TEST GARDEN

Map 2; enter off SW Rose Garden Way, West Hills;
///sank.common.fires; www.portland.gov/parks

Of course this garden is on the list: as Portland's nickname is the "City of Roses", how could it not be? At the turn of the 20th century, this flower was so popular that the city boasted a mind-boggling

Shh!

Wisteria-clad bridges, winding stone steps, and paths that disappear into the undergrowth: it sounds like something from *The Secret Garden*, right? Well, that's exactly what Elk Rock Garden feels like *(www. elkrockgarden.org)*. Nestled among the leafy streets of the city's Deep Southwest, this Scottish-style garden (built by passionate amateur gardener Peter Kerr) is a hidden hideaway for clued-up locals, who come here to wander beneath the pines and cedars.

200 miles (322 km) of rose-bordered streets – hence the nickname. Locals are still partial to a rose today and will take any excuse to visit this bloom-filled spot, whether for a picnic lunch or a birthday bash.

» Don't leave without admiring the pink Madame Caroline Testout, the breed of rose that lined the city's streets in the early 20th century.

MILL ENDS

Map 1; 56 SW Taylor Street, Downtown; ///dates.teeth.person

Blink and you'll miss it: Mill Ends is the world's smallest park (it doesn't even hit 3.5 sq ft/0.3 sq m). The most remarkable thing about it, though? It's home to a colony of leprechauns – well, according to Dick Fagan. In the 1940s, this Irish-born journalist, bent on brightening up the strip dividing two lanes of traffic near his office, planted some flowers in an unused lamppost space. His popular column about the leprechauns who lived here tickled Portlanders and Mill Ends soon became a hit. A tree and a cloverleaf border may have replaced the blooms, but this tiny park (and its inhabitants) are still Portland icons.

LAN SU CHINESE GARDEN

Map 1; 239 NW Everett Street, Old Town/Chinatown;
///loud.broken.turned; www.lansugarden.org

This Ming-style garden is an oasis of calm in the bustle of Old Town/Chinatown. Join lunching Downtown workers as they meander past lily-filled waterways and stroll under lantern-strung pagodas. Want to learn more? The tours are excellent, covering everything from the garden's bamboo to its bridges.

Dreamy Viewpoints

Of course Portland is awash with epic views –
it's encircled by countless hills, after all. Climb
high to witness the sun set and rise over the
city's stunning skyline.

JOSEPH WOOD HILL PARK

Map 6; enter at NE 92nd Avenue and NE Rocky Butte Road,
Madison South; ///pots.certified.safety;
www.portland.gov/parks/rocky-butte-natural-area

It's a bit of a jaunt from Portland's heart, but nowhere can beat Joseph
Wood Hill Park on a clear day. Perched atop Rocky Butte, a volcanic
cinder cone, this tiny park offers epic views of the Cascade Range,
including the dramatic caved-in caldera of Mount St. Helens *(p177)*.
Local life is on full display here, too: dog owners watch their pups
run wild, families picnic on the grass, and neighbors play frisbee.

MOCKS CREST PARK

Map 6; enter at end of N Skidmore Court, Overlook; ///port.crate.singer

A green lawn dotted with a few seats and trees; as a park, Mocks
Crest is pretty modest. And yet don't be fooled. Just before sunset
this grassy stretch becomes crowded with gooey-eyed couples and

friends smoking weed, all waiting for the show to begin. And what a show it is: the sun makes the Willamette glow gold before dipping below the West Hills and lighting up the sky with reds, oranges, and purples. Turn your camera to sunset mode and take it in.

ST. JOHNS BRIDGE

Map 6; enter at N Eddison Street, Cathedral Park;
///quaint.internal.fracture; www.portland.gov/parks/cathedral-park

Portland's most photographed sight? Well, the curved archways at the base of this soaring, pale-green suspension bridge must be in the running. Social-media mavens and newly engaged couples descend on leafy Cathedral Park to snap pics through the cathedral-like arches (hence the name of the park) as they disappear into the distance. Be prepared to get your elbows out if you want a shot – it gets busy.

» Don't leave without checking out the small sandy beach beneath the arched pillars of the bridge. It's a great place for a paddle.

EASTBANK ESPLANADE

Map 3; enter at SE Caruthers Street, Hosford-Abernethy;
///slice.shady.fleet; www.portland.gov/parks/eastbank-esplanade

Proving that gorgeous views aren't always found on high is this pretty waterside path, which runs beside the Willamette River, from Tilikum Crossing to Steel Bridge. Take a stroll along it to enjoy epic views of the Downtown Portland skyline and the city's famous bridges. On hot days you might spot swimsuit-clad locals lounging on (and diving off) the Holman Dock, a wooden pier near Hawthorne Bridge.

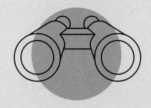

Liked by the locals

"As a performance artist and musician, I spend a lot of time in the city's parks. They provide a welcoming space where people can enjoy a range of activities, whether that's slackline walking, unicycle riding, or just taking in the view."

BRIAN KIDD, AKA THE UNIPIPER, PORTLAND'S OWN
BAGPIPING UNICYCLIST AND LOCAL CELEBRITY

MOUNT TABOR PARK

Map 5; enter at SE Salmon Street and SE 63rd Avenue, Mount Tabor;
///maps.doors.type; www.portland.gov/parks/mt-tabor-park

Every morning, fitness-focused locals get their hearts pumping by jogging or biking up Mount Tabor. Their reward? The stunning views from the crest of this volcanic cinder cone. Make for the top (jogging is optional), grab a bench, and look out across southeast Portland; from here, the city's busy boulevards look like tiny toy roads.

COUNCIL CREST PARK

Map 6; enter at SW Fairmount Boulevard and SW Talbot Terrace, West
Hills; ///keeps.insist.sofa; www.portland.gov/parks/council-crest-park

Yes, this park is a bit off the beaten path. But at 1,073 ft (328 m) high, it's also one of the loftiest points in Portland – meaning good views are guaranteed. The city's forested west side spools out below, while five peaks of the Cascades (Mount Hood among them) sit on the horizon.
» Don't leave without admiring the joyful statue of a mother and child embracing. It was sculpted by Portland art professor Frederick Littman.

POWELL BUTTE NATURE PARK

Map 6; end of SE 162 Avenue, Pleasant Valley; ///issued.hills.port;
www.friendsofpowellbutte.org

Mountain peaks are well and good, but some of Portland's best views are found closer to the ground – in this pristine park, at least. In spring, the fruit trees here are heavy with blossoms, and in summer the grass meadows brim with wildflowers. It's a pop of color you won't forget.

Alfresco Activities

Portlanders are never far from sandy shores, forested parks, and – of course – the Willamette River. The result? There's plenty of opportunity for an outdoor adventure – even on the rainiest of days.

DISC GOLF IN PIER PARK

Map 6; enter at N Bruce Avenue and N James Street, St. Johns; ///concern.sedative.splashes; www.portland.gov/parks/pier-park

A fan of frisbee? It's time to level up with a round of disc golf. Similar to club-and-ball golf, this offbeat sport swaps in a frisbee and basket. Pier Park is a good spot to try it out: the course here is one of the best in Oregon – out-of-town disc-golf obsessives will happily make the journey to have a game here – and winds beneath some sky-high Douglas firs. Oh, and there's also no fee to play.

STROLL BROUGHTON BEACH

Map 6; enter off NE Marine Drive, Northeast Portland; ///frock.moves.quarrel; www.oregonmetro.gov/parks/broughton-beach

This urban beach is where it's at come summer: sunbathers lounge lazily on the sands, friends banter over BBQs, and families splash about in the river. Take it all in with a walk along the paved Marine

Hungry? Head over to nearby Salty's On the Columbia River for tasty fresh seafood and epic river views.

Drive Trail that runs parallel to the beach, while cyclists and skaters whizz past. On a clear day, you might even spy a glimpse of soaring Mount Hood. Dreamy.

SUP ON THE WILLAMETTE RIVER

Map 3; Next Adventure, 624 SE 7th Avenue, Buckman;
///long.slips.about; www.nextadventure.net

Judging by the number of boarders on the Willamette in summer, SUPing sure is popular in Portland. Best buds laugh at each other's attempts to balance as they take in the city from a new perspective – it's definitely a blast to float beneath the Hawthorne Bridge. No worries if you're new to the water: Next Adventure offers classes and guided tours to get you feeling comfortable on the board.

» Don't leave without testing your balance and your core with an SUP yoga session. (Don't worry: even experts fail to remain upright.)

CYCLE THE 40-MILE LOOP

Map 4; start at the Eastbank Esplanade next to the Steel Bridge,
Lloyd District; ///locked.length.flock; https://40mileloop.org

Okay, so the name of this bike path is a bit misleading. It's actually 140 miles (225 km) in length – and will be even longer once it's fully finished. It is a loop though, one that encircles a huge area around the city, winding past everything from forested hills to sandy beaches. Pros can tackle it in a single go, but for those of us without thighs of steel, the riverside stretch through the city center is enough for one day.

Solo, Pair, Crowd

There are so many more ways to get active in Portland – with new friends, just the two of you, or with the whole gang.

FLYING SOLO
Make a new friend
From late June to mid-September, Portland's Fitness in the Park program sees everything from dance to tai chi classes take place in parks across the city. You'll soon get chatting with a new friend.

IN A PAIR
Rackets and roses
Washington Park's tennis courts are the perfect place to take your sporty date. The romantic International Rose Test Garden *(p166)* is next door, too. Game, set, and match.

FOR A CROWD
Team challenge
Grab your jogging-obsessed buddies and explore massive Forest Park *(p165)*. The hilly Wildwood Trail, which snakes for 29.5 miles (47 km) through deep-green forest, makes for a great group challenge.

TAKE A DIP AT POET'S BEACH

Map 6; enter at end of S Hall Street, Downtown; ///chips.swear.ahead; www.portlandoregon.gov/parks/73880

Tucked away next to the Marquam Bridge, this sandy spot is a great place for a swim. In fact, it became Portland's first official swimming area back in 2014, thanks to the hard work of the Human Access Project. This grassroots organization – set up by keen local swimmer Willie Levenson – helped get the beach in tip-top shape, adding a path and a marked swimming area for easier access. Today, the beach buzzes on sunny weekends: kids paddle by the shore while their parents chill out on the sand, and groups of friends bob about in the water. Don some swimmers and join them for a refreshing (read: chilly) dip.

» Don't leave without reading the stones by the path engraved with children's poetry and Chinook words; it's how the beach got its name.

KAYAK THE SMITH AND BYBEE WETLANDS NATURAL AREA

Map 6; 5327 N Marine Drive, North Portland; ///loud.spider.elder; www.oregonmetro.gov/parks/smith-and-bybee-wetlands-natural-area

It's hard to believe, but among the warehouses and port terminals of North Portland there lies an enchanting wildlife-filled wetland. A paddle here feels a world away from the city: as you glide past thickets of willow, the air is filled with the tweet and twitter of countless birds and the water's surface might be disturbed by an otter here and a beaver there. To enjoy it, all you need to do is rent a kayak from Cascade Paddle Rentals and get paddling.

Nearby Getaways

The stunning natural beauty of the Pacific Northwest is right on Portland's doorstep. This, plus the cute towns scattered across Oregon, means Portlanders are spoiled for choice when it comes to day trips.

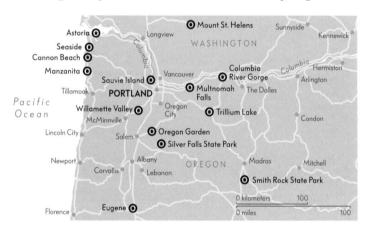

ASTORIA

2-hour drive from the city; www.astoria.or.us

There's plenty more to do in this funky little fishing town than gawk at the house from *The Goonies* (though it's fine if that's all you've got planned). Our suggestion? Tackle the 164 steps of the Astoria Column, a soaring, mural-covered tower that offers stunning views of the city and the mighty Columbia River as it flows into the Pacific. The climb is enough to work up a thirst, so it's handy there are plenty of home-grown breweries here. Have a cold one at Buoy Brewing, then grab a plate of fish and chips (beer-battered, of course) from Bowpicker.

» Don't leave without visiting Cathedral Tree, a huge 300-year-old Sitka spruce, found just a short walk from the Astoria Column.

SAUVIE ISLAND

30-minute drive from the city; www.sauvieisland.org

Sandy beaches, quaint farmland, and glittering lakes: Sauvie Island is a bucolic microcosm of the Oregon countryside. Even better, it's just a breezy 30-minute drive from Downtown Portland (via the Sauvie Island Bridge). Come summer, work-weary locals flock to the island to spend the day cycling country roads or sunbathing on the pristine sands. In fall, the island belongs to young families, who visit for cutesy activities like corn mazes and pumpkin-patch photoshoots.

MOUNT ST. HELENS

2-hour drive from the city; www.visitmtsthelens.com

Hikers heart Mount St. Helens. This active volcano (which last erupted in 1980) is a trekker's paradise, with over 200 miles (322 km) of trails. Easygoing strollers make their way past tranquil lakes and wildflower-dusted meadows, while expert trampers descend into gorges or tackle the (oh-so tiring) climb to the summit. Don't miss Ape Cave, a hollowed-out lava tunnel that's pretty easy to explore (just remember to bring a flashlight, warm clothes, and comfy shoes).

OREGON GARDEN

50-minute drive from the city; www.oregongarden.org

Come the weekend, green-fingered Portlanders make for this pretty oasis to get inspiration for their own gardens – and there's plenty of it to be had. Why? Because this 80-acre (32-ha) swath of botanical bliss isn't just one garden, it's made up of 20, including a demo garden specifically designed to inspire home horticulturists.

» Don't leave without visiting Gordon House, located in the gardens; it was designed by the famous architect Frank Lloyd Wright.

SILVER FALLS STATE PARK

1.5-hour drive from the city; https://stateparks.oregon.gov

Chasing waterfalls is something of a pastime for Oregonians. The state is home to over 200 cascades, many of which can be found in leafy Silver Falls State Park. Set off on the park's Trail of Ten Falls,

Many of the sandy stretches lining the Oregon coast can feel a bit busy (we're looking at you Cannon Beach). But Short Sands (aka Shorty's to locals) tends to be miraculously quiet, apart from a couple of surfers. Maybe that's because reaching this pristine beach, found in Oswald West State Park, requires a short walk from a parking lot just off Highway 101. Enclosed by dramatic cliffs and tall cedar trees, it's a great place to vibe out on a blanket while the sun sets over the ocean.

which (as you'd expect) passes by ten stunning waterfalls, including the 175-ft- (53-m) high South Falls. The coolest thing? The path laces around the back of this fall, so you can glimpse the thundering torrent from behind.

CANNON BEACH

1.5-hour drive from the city; www.cannonbeach.org

There are so many reasons to love this bustling town – but the main one is its sandy shoreline. Hugging the edge of the Pacific, this wide stretch of golden beach is beloved by an eclectic crowd: gangs of surfers ride the waves here during the day, while in the evening aspiring photographers snap sunset shots of Haystack Rock for their socials. (This massive rock formation has featured in several movies, including, you guessed it, *The Goonies*.) Sand aside, this lively town is also crammed with local art galleries and top-notch brewpubs.

SMITH ROCK STATE PARK

3-hour drive from the city; www.smithrock.com

Hailed as the birthplace of US sport climbing, Smith Rock is a magnet for intrepid climbers. Around 2,000 routes (which are permanently bolted to the stone) snake up the park's rugged basalt spires, luring the adventurous to go sky high. For those who aren't stoked on getting vertical, there's a wide variety of camping and hiking options nearby, including the laid-back Rim Rock Trail. This easy half-mile (1-km) stroll along a canyon ridge offers awesome views of the park's craggy scenery – all with your feet firmly on the ground.

MULTNOMAH FALLS

30-minute drive from the city; www.multnomahfallslodge.com

Some claim that South Falls in Silver Falls State Park *(p178)* is the best waterfall in Oregon, but this two-tier cascade can definitely give it a run for its money. Get ready to gawp as this ribbon of water tumbles 611 ft (186 m) down a rock face, flows beneath the forest-fringed Benson Bridge, and then rushes another 100 ft (30 m) into a deep pool. Come during winter or spring to catch it at its most powerful and most spectacular.

EUGENE

2-hour drive from the city; www.eugenecascadescoast.org

Sure, San Francisco played a key role in the counterculture boom, but it wasn't the only spot on the West Coast to do so. This leafy town (home of the writer and psychedelic pioneer Ken Kesey) was an important co-conspirator in the hippie movement – and not much has changed since the 1960s. Locals still wander around in Birkenstocks and tie-dye outfits; you can't throw a rock without hitting a cannabis dispensary; and you're never more than a block or two from a veggie or vegan restaurant.

TRILLIUM LAKE

1.5-hour drive from the city

This glacier-fed lake is about as good looking as a lake can get. Surrounded by tall green pines, the mirror-like waters glisten with the reflection of snowcapped Mount Hood, which looms high above the landscape. Portlanders pining for a dose of nature head for the popular campground found on the edge of the lake (book well in advance), and spend most of their time here simply admiring the awe-inspiring view.

» Don't leave without visiting nearby Timberline Lodge. This National Historic Landmark served as the exterior of the Overlook Hotel in 1980 horror film *The Shining*.

SEASIDE

1.5-hour drive from the city; www.seasideor.com

This charmingly tacky coastal town is the closest thing Oregon has to an East Coast-style seaside village – and Portlanders love it. Here you'll find neon-lit arcades, ice-cream parlors, cute gift shops, and, of course, a beautiful sandy beach. In summer, stylish couples dressed in their best stroll arm-in-arm along "The Prom" (the town's long oceanfront promenade), while friends scoff bags of saltwater taffy – the town has enough of this candy to keep all of Oregon high on sugar for months.

Try it!
BEACH CLEANS

Keep Seaside's shore free of trash by grabbing a beach cleanup bag from the aquarium. As well as doing your bit for the environment, you'll earn "cleanup coins" which can be used at participating local coffee shops.

Liked by the locals

"Manzanita is about 15 minutes farther from Portland by car than Seaside or Cannon Beach. That's just enough to filter out the tourists and keep this charming little village, with its unique public beach and breathtaking mountain views, for locals who know better."

CHRIS ANGELUS, HOST OF RIGHT AT THE FORK PODCAST

WILLAMETTE VALLEY

40-minute drive from the city; www.willamettevalley.org

Let's get this straight: the Napa Valley might be famous, but it isn't alone in cultivating kick-ass US wines. Enter the Willamette Valley, whose fertile hills have been producing world-beating vintages for generations. Take a tour of its vineyards (there are over 500) and sample some of its dreamy pinot noirs. By the end we guarantee you'll be saying "Napa what now?"

COLUMBIA RIVER GORGE

1-hour drive from the city; www.columbiarivergorge.info

This monumental river canyon is Portland's ultimate adventure playground. Adrenaline-seeking locals come here to cycle the winding tarmac roads, hike along dramatic ridges, or windsurf on the mighty Columbia River. The best thing, though? The gorge's belt of small towns are famed for their homegrown breweries and farm-fresh food – making them the perfect place to indulge after a day on the go.

» Don't leave without stopping at Crown Point, a 733-ft- (223-m-) high basalt promontory that offers stunning views over the gorge.

MANZANITA

2-hour drive from the city; www.exploremanzanita.com

The Oregon coast's towns can feel hectic come summer – but not this sleepy little spot. Join savvy Portlanders and laid-back Manzanita locals as they stroll along the near-deserted beach or kick back in one of the town's cute cafés. Just keep it on the down-low, yeah?

OLD
TOWN

NORTHWEST

Enter the park at the
JAPANESE AMERICAN
HISTORICAL PLAZA

This cherry-tree-dotted plaza is home to 13 stone markers. They commemorate the history of the 120,000 Japanese Americans deported to internment camps during World War II.

2

Taking place beneath the Burnside Bridge, the Portland Saturday Market is packed with over 250 vendors selling locally made wares.

WEST BURNSIDE STREET

Burnside Bridge

I-5

Begin the day at
SIMPLE. LOCAL. COFFEE

Fuel up with a chai latte and a freshly made stuffed bagel sandwich at this cute coffee shop.

1

SOUTHWEST WASHINGTON STREET

DOWNTOWN

SOUTHWEST ALDER STREET

NAITO PARKWAY

WILLAMETTE GREENWAY TRAIL

3

Check out the exhibits in the
OREGON MARITIME
MUSEUM

Learn all about Portland's maritime and shipbuilding past at this fun museum, which is housed in a historic steam-powered tug boat.

SOUTHWEST

Morrison Bridge

Look out for
MILL ENDS

A short stroll away, this diminutive spot is the smallest park in the world; it is purportedly home to a colony of leprechauns.

4

SOUTHWEST MADISON STREET

Willamette River

The dramatic, twin-spired Hawthorne Bridge is the oldest in Portland, and the oldest vertical lift bridge in the US.

SOUTHWEST

SW NAITO PARKWAY

Hawthorne Bridge

I-5

SOUTHEAST MARTIN LUTHER KING JUNIOR BOULEVARD

Kick back at
LITTLE RIVER CAFE

Reward yourself for all that walking with lunch at this artsy spot offering views over the boat-filled harbor.

5

| 0 meters | 200 |
| 0 yards | 200 |

NORTHEAST

EAST BURNSIDE STREET

BUCKMAN

SOUTHEAST STARK STREET

SOUTHEAST MORRISON STREET

SOUTHEAST

SOUTHEAST HAWTHORNE BLVD

HOSFORD-
ABERNETHY

A morning exploring
Waterfront Park

It's hard to believe, but in the 1960s this leafy riverside park was a six-lane highway. That all changed in 1969, when community organizers held a series of picnics on the narrow pedestrian walkway here, as a way of petitioning for more public space. The event convinced the then Oregon Governor Tom McCall, who replaced the freeway with a public park. Today, this green stretch is a favorite with locals, who come here for laid-back strolls along the riverfront.

1. Simple. Local. Coffee
115 SW Ash Street,
Downtown; www.simple
localcoffeepdx.com
///learns.librarian.driver

**2. Japanese American
Historical Plaza**
2 NW Naito Parkway,
Downtown
///nights.market.lights

3. Oregon Maritime Museum
198 SW Naito Parkway,
Downtown; www.oregon
maritimemuseum.org
///richer.seated.late

4. Mill Ends
SW Taylor Street, Downtown
///dates.teeth.person

5. Little River Cafe
315 S Montgomery
Street #310, Downtown;
www.littlerivercafe.com
///plots.ticket.secret

**Portland Saturday
Market**
///trying.data.picked

Hawthorne Bridge
///rare.socket.cheek

With a little research and preparation, this city will feel like a home away from home. Check out these websites to ensure a healthy, safe stay in Portland.

Portland
DIRECTORY

SAFE SPACES
Portland is known for being a liberal city, but should you feel uneasy or want to find your community, there are spaces and resources to help you out.

www.gaypdx.com
A directory listing LGBTQ+-friendly spaces, as well as support organizations and resources.

www.iloveblackfood.com/ pdx-directory
A curated list of Black-owned restaurants, cafés, and bars in Portland; it includes a useful map.

www.pdxqcenter.org
Q Center is the largest LGBTQ+ community and resource center in the Pacific Northwest.

www.travelportland.com/culture
The city's official tourist website has useful information and resources for Portland's various religious and cultural communities.

HEALTH
Health care in the US isn't free, so it's important to take out comprehensive health insurance for your visit. If you do need medical assistance, there are many pharmacies and hospitals across the city.

www.multco.us/health/health-services
The official website for Multnomah (the county Portland resides within) has a list of the area's health and dental clinics.

www.plannedparenthood.org/ health-center/oregon/portland
Nonprofit organization providing sexual health care for all.

www.walgreens.com
Store locator showing 24-hour and late-night Walgreens pharmacies.

www.zoomcare.com
Portland's own local chain of affordable health care clinics, offering an alternative to emergency rooms.

TRAVEL SAFETY INFORMATION
Before you travel – and while you're here – always keep tabs on the latest regulations in Portland, and the US.

www.cdc.gov
National public health institute offering disease prevention and guidance.

www.travelportland.com/plan/ safety-in-portland
Regular safety updates on Portland, with information on crime, protests, COVID-19, police activity, and other concerns.

https://govstatus.egov.com/ OR-OHA-COVID-19
Oregon's official COVID-19 website with information, updates, and resources.

https://stateparks.oregon.gov
Official site for Oregon's state parks, with information on weather and hazards.

www.travel.state.gov
Latest travel safety information from the US government.

ACCESSIBILITY
Portland is often hailed as an accessible city, with most venues and services available to all people. These resources will help make your journeys go smoothly.

www.acb.org
National organization providing resources and support to blind and partially sighted people.

www.portland.gov/civic/disability/ accessible-travel
The city government site offers a list of tips and resources for navigating the city.

www.traillink.com
Highlights wheelchair-accessible trails around Oregon.

www.trimet.org/access/index.htm
The city's public transportation provider offers accessibility information for Portland's buses and trains.

www.willamettepartnership.org/ accessible-travel-guide
An accessible travel guide for exploring Oregon's great outdoors.

INDEX

ABOUT THE ILLUSTRATOR

Mantas Tumosa

Creative designer and illustrator Mantas moved from his home country of Lithuania to London back in 2011. By day, he's busy creating bold, minimalistic illustrations that tell a story – such as the gorgeous cover of this book. By night, he's dreaming of adventures away, catching up on the basketball, and cooking Italian food (which he can't get enough of).

Main Contributors Alexander Frane, Jennifer Moore, Peter Cottell

Senior Editor Lucy Richards

Senior Designers Tania Gomes, Ben Hinks, Stuti Tiwari Bhatia

Project Editor Rachel Laidler

Editor Elspeth Beidas

Designer Jordan Lambley

Proofreader Kathryn Glendenning

Senior Cartographic Editor Casper Morris

Cartography Manager Suresh Kumar

Cartographer Ashif

Jacket Designers Tania Gomes, Jordan Lambley

Jacket Illustrator Mantas Tumosa

Senior Production Editor Jason Little

Senior Production Controller Samantha Cross

Managing Editor Hollie Teague

Managing Art Editor Sarah Snelling

Art Director Maxine Pedliham

Publishing Director Georgina Dee

A NOTE FROM DK EYEWITNESS

The world is fast-changing and it's keeping us folk at DK Eyewitness on our toes. We've worked hard to ensure that this edition of Portland Like a Local is up-to-date and reflects today's favorite places but we know that standards shift, venues close, and new ones pop up in their place. So, if you notice something has closed, we've got something wrong, or left something out, we want to hear about it. Please drop us a line at travelguides@dk.com

First edition 2022

Published in Great Britain by Dorling Kindersley Limited, DK, One Embassy Gardens, 8 Viaduct Gardens, London SW11 7BW, UK

The authorised representative in the EEA is Dorling Kindersley Verlag GmbH. Arnulfstr. 124, 80636 Munich, Germany

DK Publishing, 1745 Broadway, 20th Floor, New York, NY 10019, USA

Copyright © 2022 Dorling Kindersley Limited
A Penguin Random House Company
22 23 24 25 10 9 8 7 6 5 4 3 2 1

A CIP catalog record for this book is available from the British Library.

A catalog record for this book is available from the Library of Congress.

ISSN: 1542 1554
ISBN: 978 0 2415 6828 6

Printed and bound in China.

www.dk.com